A Discourse on African Philosophy

African Philosophy:
Critical Perspectives and Global Dialogue

Series Editor: Uchenna B. Okeja, Rhodes University; and Bruce B. Janz, University of Central Florida

Editorial Board: Anthony Appiah, Valentine Mudimbe, Gail Presbey, Achille Mbembe, Robert Bernasconi, Samuel Imbo, Tsenay Serequeberhan, Thaddeus Metz, Katrin Flikschuh, Niels Weidtmann, Christine Wanjiru Gichure, Kai Kresse, Joseph Agbakoba, Souleymane Bachir Diagne, Dismas. A. Masolo, Pedro Tabensky

The *African Philosophy: Critical Perspectives and Global Dialogue* book series aims to promote emerging critical perspectives in different branches of African philosophy. It serves as an avenue for philosophers within and between many African cultures to present new arguments, ask new questions, and begin new dialogues within both specialized communities and with the general public. By merging the critical and global dimensions of thoughts pertaining to important topics in African philosophy, this series beams the lights and rigour of philosophical analysis on topical as well as classical questions reflective of the African and African diaspora search for meaning in existence. Focused on the best of African philosophy, the series will introduce new concepts and new approaches in philosophy both to intellectual communities across Africa, as well as the rest of the world.

Titles in the Series

A Discourse on African Philosophy: A New Perspective on Ubuntu *and Transitional Justice in South Africa,* by Christian B. N. Gade

Disentangling Consciencism*: Essays on Kwame Nkrumah's Philosophy,* edited by Martin Odei Ajei

The Rule of Law and Governance in Indigenous Yoruba Society: An Essay in African Philosophy of Law, by John Ayotunde Isola Bewaji

A Discourse on African Philosophy

A New Perspective on Ubuntu *and Transitional Justice in South Africa*

Christian B. N. Gade
Foreword by Michael Onyebuchi Eze

LEXINGTON BOOKS
Lanham • Boulder • New York • London

Published by Lexington Books
An imprint of The Rowman & Littlefield Publishing Group, Inc.
4501 Forbes Boulevard, Suite 200, Lanham, Maryland 20706
www.rowman.com

Unit A, Whitacre Mews, 26-34 Stannary Street, London SE11 4AB

Copyright © 2017 by Lexington Books

All rights reserved. No part of this book may be reproduced in any form or by any electronic or mechanical means, including information storage and retrieval systems, without written permission from the publisher, except by a reviewer who may quote passages in a review.

British Library Cataloguing in Publication Information Available

Library of Congress Cataloging-in-Publication Data
The hardback edition of this book was previously cataloged by the Library of Congress as follows:

Names: Gade, Christian B. N., author.
Title: A discourse on African philosophy : a new perspective on Ubuntu and transitional justice in South Africa / Christian B.N. Gade ; foreword by Michael Onyebuchi Eze.
Description: Lanham : Lexington Books, 2017. | Series: African philosophy: critical perspectives and global dialogue | Includes bibliographical references and index.
Identifiers: LCCN 2017002424 (print) | LCCN 2017008465 (ebook)
Subjects: LCSH: Ubuntu (Philosophy) | Transitional justice--South Africa. | South Africa. Truth and Reconciliation Commission. | Reconciliation--Political aspects--South Africa.
Classification: LCC B5315.U28 G33 2017 (print) | LCC B5315.U28 (ebook) | DDC 199/.6--dc23 LC record available at https://lccn.loc.gov/2017002424

ISBN 978-1-4985-1225-1 (cloth : alk. paper)
ISBN 978-1-4985-1227-5 (pbk. : alk. paper)
ISBN 978-1-4985-1226-8 (Electronic)

To my beloved family

The future depends on how we relate to the past

Table of Contents

Foreword ... ix
    Michael Onyebuchi Eze
Acknowledgments ... xiii

1	Introduction	1
2	African Philosophy for Change	9
3	Transitional Justice in South Africa	19
4	The South African TRC and *Ubuntu*	29
5	Ethnophilosophy: The Myth of Shared Static Ideas	47
6	The Diversity and Development of *Ubuntu* Ideas	55
7	*Ubuntu*, History, and Politics	77
8	Postscript	89

Bibliography ... 91
Index ... 99
About the Author ... 105

Foreword

Michael Onyebuchi Eze

Christian Gade, in this excellent discourse on African philosophy, offers a new perspective on the role of *ubuntu* and the Truth and Reconciliation Commission (TRC) in the making of modern South Africa. He does not accept the tendency evident in much of the literature to ignore the role of history and social context in the making of new national culture or political imagination. As so often in times of national reconstruction, cultural enterprises come to be expressive of national character.

Ubuntu was employed by the post-apartheid South African government to construct a new political imagination, one that would displace the old apartheid order. Its creative use in academic discourse has produced a new vision of history in which the past is no longer a location of subjective alienation or exclusion, but a source of sociopolitical and moral unity. *Ubuntu* has become a prophetic moral national culture in which all South Africans, irrespective of race, find a home. The emotional legitimacy that it evokes accounts both for its arbitrary use and even for its commodification in the TRC and thereafter. Yet precisely because it was not historicized, *ubuntu* has initiated new points of contestation within the field of African philosophy. In this context, it becomes a magic discourse with an eccentric blend of characteristics:

1. A retrograde tradition that eschews history and context in favor of cultural essentialism;
2. An ideological discourse imposed as a conscious imagination with the potential to cure post-apartheid South Africa of all melancholies and anxieties from the past;
3. Being ideological means also that it is essentially exclusive, drawing its practitioners into an ethno-consciousness reflecting primarily the victor's morality and justice;
4. Without being historicized, *ubuntu* also reads as a dogma, functioning albeit subjective conversion of historical experiences;[1]
5. As a system of thought, *ubuntu* evokes exotic complexities: an epistemic proof for supremacy of African values; a source of validation for African philosophy; a "displacement narrative" to apartheid discourse; a "reactionary discourse" or elitist project of professional philosophers.[2]

The challenge here is that if *ubuntu* does indeed emerge as a displacement narrative, then it cannot authentically claim to be a true African philosophy, for it remains a project of the Other, that is, invented in the colonial gaze. It becomes merely a residual narrative. The African philosopher practicing such discourse is entrapped in what may be termed the "colonization of subjectivity."[3] The philosophical enterprise itself only gains essence as a response to Western historical episteme. Seen as a reactionary discourse, *ubuntu* philosophy is afflicted with the same disease it is hoped to cure, an essentialist rendered discourse possessing all the homogeneous credentials of the old apartheid order without any room for difference or innovation.

Gade is mindful of these limitations as evident in his criticism of the project of African philosophy. Closely following the writing of Paulin Hountondji, Gade criticizes earlier studies in the discipline now termed "ethnophilosophy." Hountondji has criticized what he terms ethnophilosophy as nurtured by narratives of historical mystification, unanimity and cultural essentialism:

> Our position on this point is materialist: philosophy is above all a cultural fact with an objective social existence, and it must be approached empirically rather than postulated, like the sedative power of opium, as the conclusion of a process of induction. . . . Ethnophilosophers neglect this plurality, this irreducible polysemy of discourses. They impoverish African literature by reducing all the genres to one and by giving its infinite variety a single metaphysical common denominator.[4]

Ethnophilosophy casts African philosophy as a response to European colonial historicity. The African philosophers for their part become, in the writing of Okot P'Bitek, "mercenaries in foreign battles, none of which was in the interest of the African peoples . . . intellectual smugglers."[5] The African philosopher exists only to satisfy the curiosity of the Western mind through intellectual mimicry. He/she philosophizes to offer proofs or certificates of humanity to the Western audience, which remains the largest consumer of such knowledge production.

The Belgian Franciscan, Placide Tempels, is often cast as the highwater mark of that tradition of ethnophilosophy. Tempels wrote *Bantu Philosophy* to counter the intellectual racism of European historicity which gave justification for colonialism and for the dehumanization of blacks. According to this logic of colonialism, in simple terms, the very act of colonialism is a charitable affair. The Enlightenment had redeemed the European soul from the oppressive structures of the monarchy and the Church. From the Enlightenment, Westerners had learned that humanity is dependent neither on the divine right of kings nor on the mercy of the Church. Rationality was what endows humanity. But this rationality was not universal. Non-Westerners had no such benefit, yet through colonialism might acquire humanity through special education (assimilation, association, or assimilado). They might thus become human, and begin to reason like the white man.[6]

Tempels' work was an attempt to respond to this logic and to give a voice to the African subject so diminished by the colonial logic. Perhaps if he could prove that the African had a logical system of thought like the European, there might be a chance for subjective equality between the Bantu and the European. If this Bantu were to be recognized as a rational being, this would undercut the justifications given to dehumanize and colonize him. The quarrel is not with Tempels' motivation—which, in my view, was noble. The main weakness was his methodology, which conceived of African philosophy as merely a residual narrative to European philosophy. To be recognized as an equal human being, the African must philosophize or think like the European.

Gade is aware of these shortfalls in ethnophilosophy. Gade's book echoes Hountondji's call for empirical study of African philosophy. In addition to history, Gade also employs anthropological method and this offers him a leeway for a creative rehabilitation of *ubuntu* and African philosophy in general. This intellectual, sympathy, however, needs to be qualified. *Ubuntu* must be read within history. *Ubuntu* is useful but must be read as relevant to context. A view I equally share that goods are internal to the practices of a community. The legitimacy of *ubuntu* is not because it is an inherited cultural value or because it is said to constitute a people's cultural history. *Ubuntu* is validated on what it offers to our immediate sociopolitical predicament and circumstances. History and social context are the non-negotiable prerequisite for cultural history. In the case of *ubuntu*, the shift away from an essentialist rendered definition to performative discourse exhibits a vertical+horizontal appendage. It is a method that empowers us to become actors, agents, and subjects of history and not only objects of history. The method appropriates both a linear account of history as well as other multiple influences (bias, prejudices, mindsets, stereotypes) present at the point of our historical configuration.[7] Context speaks to history but history is informed and nourished by our immediate social experiences. For Gade, history and context equally play key roles in cultural history. The immediate need is the recognition of *ubuntu* as a public good or source of moral unity which all South Africans can recognize as good. This lies at the foundation of Gade's call for rehabilitation of African philosophical thinking and indeed a courageous project. African Philosophy must be meaningful and courageous too. It must address issues of the most vivid concern affecting Africa. It must be courageous in its attempt to find its own voice, to resonate with its social and historical context. It must not be a mimicry of antiquated but irrelevant traditions. It must move away from being merely a residual narrative of European intellectual consciousness.

In Gade's reference to Nietzsche's antiquarian history, we are offered a creative impulse of historical ideology for positive change. However, history must not constitute a nihilist obsession. We must study the African past, but not as a crutch to social progress, with history becoming a location of the disquiet, a "battle axe" that continues to haunt the people. There is recognition that we need to move away from essentialist rendered understanding, which not only obfuscates the genuine contribution of *ubuntu* to legitimate political change, but projects it as a closed system of values.

This work is a formidable thesis for a new thinking on African philosophy. The author maps new ways of thinking about African philosophy that are not entrapped by the mystifications of the past. As a historian of culture and social change, naturally I agree with him. In the language of Hountondji, African philosophy must be freed from the "fetishism" of unanimity or historicism. Its entrapment by the past as a locus of epistemic truth renders no service to African philosophical studies. Gade concludes by calling for "differences, historical developments and social contexts" to speak to us. What is indeed creative here is that double deployment of both historical and anthropological methods in shedding light on the perennial questions and vexing problems of African philosophy.

This new addition to the literature on African political thought is a welcome respite to those who read and write about African philosophy. Its subject is the influence of history in the making of modern African identity, nationalism, peace-building, and questions of justice.

Michael Onyebuchi Eze, PhD
Trinity Hall
University of Cambridge

NOTES

1. See Michael Onyebuchi Eze, *Intellectual History in Contemporary South Africa* (New York: Palgrave Macmillan, 2010), 57, 190.
2. For a detailed discussion on *ubuntu* as a critique of colonial/apartheid logic, see Eze, *Intellectual History in Contemporary South Africa*, pp. 119–43.
3. Ibid, 29, 187–89.
4. Pauline Hountondji, *African Philosophy: Myth and Reality*. Second Edition. Translated by Henri Evans and Jonathan Rée (Bloomington: Indiana University Press, 1996), 176, 179.
5. Okot P'Bitek, *African Religions in Western Scholarship* (Nairobi: Kenya Literature Bureau, 1971), 102, 107.
6. Women were equally disregarded.
7. For detailed discussion on this, see also, Eze, *Intellectual History in Contemporary South Africa*, 150.

Acknowledgments

I have learned so much from the people in South Africa who have told me about their understandings of *ubuntu* and the TRC, and I want to thank all of them for sharing their knowledge. A special thanks to Augustine Shutte, who, sadly, is no longer with us. Augustine and I discussed *ubuntu* with an unflagging interest, and he and his wife Acilia welcomed me and my family in their Cape Town home several times. This has meant the world to me. I am also grateful to colleagues in the Department of Anthropology and the Department of Philosophy and History of Ideas at Aarhus University who have commented on my research. A special thanks to Andrea Kiel Nielsen for helping me to finalize this book manuscript and for taking care of many practical publication issues. Finally, thanks to Helle for all her support. She is my love, and a rock in our family.

Christian B. N. Gade

ONE

Introduction

It has frequently been argued that *ubuntu* was a formative influence on the TRC, South Africa's famous transitional justice mechanism. Antjie Krog, a recognized South African writer on the TRC, for example characterizes *ubuntu* as "the essence and foundation of the TRC process."[1] The aim of this book is to challenge and contextualize this view in a way that not only provides new findings and reflections on *ubuntu* and the TRC, but also contributes to the field of African philosophy. One of my key findings, founded on qualitative interviews in South Africa,[2] is that some former TRC commissioners and committee members question the importance of *ubuntu* in the TRC process. Another is that there are several differing and historically developing interpretations of *ubuntu*, some of which have evident political implications and reflect non-factual and creative uses of history. Thus *ubuntu* is not a cultural heritage that is shared, in the ethnophilosophical sense of constituting a static property characterizing a group.[3] In fact, throughout this book I will argue that the ethnophilosophical approach to African philosophy as a static group property is highly problematic. My research presents an alternative collective discourse on African philosophy ("collective" in the sense that it does not focus on any single individual in particular) which takes differences, historical developments, and social contexts seriously.

Ubuntu has received considerable attention in post-apartheid South Africa. For instance, the epilogue of the South African interim constitution of 1993 states that, in addressing the strife and divisions of the apartheid past, "there is a need for understanding but not for vengeance, a need for reparation but not for retaliation, a need for *ubuntu* but not for victimization."[4] According to the South African Constitutional Court, which was established by the interim constitution to decide on constitutional matters, the appearance of the word *ubuntu* in the epilogue was neither unimportant nor coincidental. This is illustrated by the following quotations from Constitutional Court cases: "Those who negotiated the [Interim] constitution made a deliberate choice, preferring understanding over vengeance, reparation over retaliation, *ubuntu* over victimization"[5]; "The concept *ubuntu* appears for the first time in the post-amble [another name for the epilogue], but it is a concept that permeates the Constitution generally"[6]; "The spirit of *ubuntu*, part of a deep cultural heritage of the majority of the population, suffuses the whole constitutional order"[7]; "Historically it [*ubuntu*] was foundational to the spirit of reconciliation and bridge-building that enabled our deeply traumatized society to overcome and transcend the divisions of the past"[8]; "It was against the background of the loss of respect for human life and the inherent dignity which attaches to every person that a spontaneous call has arisen among sections of the community for a return to *ubuntu*."[9]

This call for a return to *ubuntu* is very relevant for understanding the post-apartheid claims about the importance of *ubuntu* in the TRC process, and therefore I begin this book by reflecting on that call. My point of departure is Kwasi Wiredu's claim that national reconstruction is a cultural enterprise of the highest kind.[10] Wiredu explains that colonialism had wounded African culture in various degrees, and that many African postcolonial leaders had a strong sense of the importance of cultural self-identity, and further were convinced that they needed to reassert their own culture and review the colonial systems from an African standpoint. Using Leonhard Praeg's notion of "narrative of return,"[11] I then demonstrate that the post-apartheid narrative of return to *ubuntu* resembles similar narratives in earlier postcolonial transition periods, including narrative about *ujamaa* in Tanzania, *consciencism* in Ghana, *négritude* in Senegal, and *hunhuims* or *ubuntuism* in Zimbabwe. An important function of these narratives has been to reassert African culture and restore the dignity and autonomy of Africans.

Having contextualized the post-apartheid call for a return to *ubuntu*, I move on to contextualize the TRC within the landscape of transitional justice. According to a frequently quoted report by former UN Secretary General Kofi Annan, the notion of transitional justice comprises "the full range of processes and mechanisms associated with a society's attempts to come to terms with a legacy of large-scale abuses, in order to assure accountability, serve justice and achieve reconciliation."[12] Such mechanisms include criminal prosecutions, reparations, institutional reforms, and truth commissions. There have been several truth commissions,[13] but the South African TRC is the only one that has incorporated a conditional amnesty process. In order to receive amnesty for gross human rights violations, each perpetrator had to make an individual amnesty application to the TRC and had to testify about his or her offense during a public hearing of the Commission's Amnesty Committee. It was a prerequisite for amnesty that the offense was politically motivated and that it was proportional to the political motive.[14] Thus perpetrators could not receive amnesty for offenses committed for personal gain or out of personal malice. Altogether, the TRC received 7,128 amnesty applications; only 849 were granted amnesty. In addition, the TRC's Human Rights Violations Committee received statements from 21,290 people, of whom about 10 percent had the chance to tell their stories during public victim hearings. There were also special hearings about the role of businesses, faith communities, political parties, etc. in the perpetration of gross human rights violations. The TRC had offices in Johannesburg, Durban, East London, and Cape Town, but held hearings at various locations around the country. Human rights violations hearings were held from April 18, 1996 to June 26, 1997; special hearings from August 17, 1996 to June 18, 1998; and amnesty hearings from May 20, 1996 to December 13, 2000. A five-volume *Report of the Truth and Reconciliation Commission* was presented to President Nelson Mandela on October 29, 1998; two additional volumes were presented to President Thabo Mbeki on March 21, 2003.[15]

In my contextualization of the TRC within the landscape of transitional justice, I explain that though the TRC laid great emphasis on truth as a road to reconciliation, the truth that the TRC presented was a partial one.[16] I also highlight that truth about the past plays differing roles in different kinds of transitional justice, and that truth-seeking processes may be related to differing notions of justice. In this context, I argue that although the TRC process has often been seen to promote restorative justice, the relationship between the TRC and restorative justice is a highly complex one. Furthermore, reflecting on Samuel P. Huntington's research on democratization, I point out that diverse types of societal transitions result in differing power structures in the post-transition societies, and that these structures may place constraints on the possibilities for transitional justice. The post-apartheid government was not free to choose whether or not to grant amnesty; amnesty was a controversial compromise that resulted from the South African negotiated settlement, and many saw the TRC amnesty process as highly problematic. Clearly, there was a need to "sell" the TRC to the public. Richard Wilson is highly aware of this need, and he argues that *ubuntu* became "the Africanist wrapping used to sell a reconciliatory version of human rights talk to black South Africans."[17] I believe Wilson is correct that *ubuntu* was used to sell the TRC process, but he neglects to inform us that there were only sporadic references to *ubuntu* in the TRC hearings, and that the references to *ubuntu* in the hearings hardly constitute a "sales project" of the TRC itself. Thus the "selling" has taken place outside the TRC and, as I will argue, often retroactively.

After contextualizing the TRC within the landscape of transitional justice, I zoom in on the role of *ubuntu* in the TRC process. First, I explore the use of the word *ubuntu* in the approximately 10,000 documents on the official TRC website. Among these documents, which include transcripts of the TRC hearings, workshop transcripts, media articles, and statements, I have found the word *ubuntu* in only fifty-four documents. This number makes me question whether *ubuntu* was really the essence and foundation of the TRC process, as claimed by Krog. In fact, my findings show that among the TRC commissioners, it was almost exclusively Desmond Tutu, the TRC chairman, who used the word *ubuntu* in TRC hearings; and even he did not use the word very often. Furthermore, when I interviewed former TRC commissioners and committee members, I was told that they did not discuss *ubuntu* and that there was no conscious attempt to implement *ubuntu* in the TRC process. For example, former TRC Commissioner Glenda Wildschut said: "We did not sit down and say: How can we do this [in the spirit of] *ubuntu*? So there was no conscious attempt to do that."[18] Nevertheless, some commissioners emphasized that specific aspects of the TRC process may be seen to reflect *ubuntu*, and that some victims demonstrated *ubuntu*, while perpetrators failed to show it.

Having presented my interview material on *ubuntu* and the TRC, I delve deeper into the issue of African philosophy, particularly the question of how philosophical ideas are shared in collectives. My point of departure is Placide Tempels' *Bantu Philosophy*, the first book on African philosophy, published in 1945. This book is also the first text in the ethnophilosophical trend in African philosophy, a trend which dominated the discipline until the emergence of other trends such as nationalist ideological philosophy in the late 1950s, philosophic sagacity in the 1970s, and professional African philosophy also in the 1970s.[19] According to Tempels, the Bantu philosophy is a property of the whole Bantu group and informs the behavior of all the Bantu people.[20] As he writes: "This universal wisdom is accepted by everyone, it is not subjected to criticism, it has currency, in regard to its general principles, as imperishable Truth."[21] I argue that Tempels' work is problematic for a number of reasons, not least methodologically from a Popperian point of view. Afterwards, I extend my critique of Tempels to a critique of ethnophilosophy more generally, and in this connection I draw on Paulin J. Hountondji's famous critique of the ethnophilosophical trend.

Historically, the critique of ethnophilosophy by Hountondji and others led to an increasing individualization of African philosophy, with the emergence of trends such as philosophic sagacity and professional philosophy, which focused respectively on the thought of individual African philosophic sages and on that of individual African professional philosophers. I believe however that it is possible to have meaningful collective approaches to African philosophy, in spite of the drawbacks associated with ethnophilosophy. In fact, as stated earlier, my research on *ubuntu* and the TRC as presented in this book illustrates an alternative collective discourse on African philosophy that takes difference, historical developments, and social contexts seriously. Rather than taking the existence of shared static ideas for granted, I engage in empirical investigation to explore whether ideas are static and shared. Methodologically, my investigation is founded on qualitative interviews and historical text investigations. There is nothing new about such methods; what is innovative is the use of these empirical methods—as used in anthropology and the study of history—in relation to African philosophy.[22]

According to my findings, some South Africans define *ubuntu* as a moral quality of a person, while others define it as a phenomenon—for instance a philosophy, an ethic, African humanism, or a worldview—according to which persons are interconnected. Furthermore, South Africans have diverse views on *who* count as persons (*abantu* in the Nguni languages). While some are of the view that all members of the *Homo sapiens* species are persons, others suggest that it is only those who are black, those who have participated in particular rituals, or those who behave within specific moral parameters, who are persons. My historical text investigation also suggests that there has been a historical development in how *ubuntu* is understood. I have traced the word *ubuntu* all the way back to nineteenth-century texts, the oldest dating from 1846—which stands in stark contrast to Wim van Binsbergen's suggestion that the oldest text on *ubuntu* is the Samkanges' book, *Hunhuims or Ubuntuism: A Zimbabwe Indigenous Political Philosophy*, which dates from 1980.[23] I show that the idea that *ubuntu* is a human quality is already found in the oldest sources, while interpretations of *ubuntu* as a philosophy, an ethic, African humanism, or as a worldview, did not appear in writing before the second half of the twentieth century. Furthermore, the widespread notion that *ubuntu* is somehow expressed by, or encapsulated in, the Nguni proverb *umuntu ngumuntu ngabantu* ("a person is a person through other persons") seems to have been articulated for the first time in the 1990s, in the context of the South African transition process after apartheid. The emphasis on *ubuntu* as being about interconnectedness between persons—understood as *all* members of the species *Homo sapiens*—means that *ubuntu* has come to serve as a political counter-ideology to the segregation ideology of the previous apartheid regime, and has thus become a powerful political tool for the post-apartheid government.

Part of the reason why *ubuntu* has become such a powerful political tool is the call for a return to *ubuntu*, a call that has arisen among sections of the South African community including, as cited above, the Constitutional Court. Thus I end the book by reviewing the call for a return to *ubuntu* and offering reflections on the historical and political dimensions of this call. In doing so, I zoom in on former President Thabo Mbeki, who has used references to the African precolonial past, and specifically references to *ubuntu*, very actively in his political project. I argue that Mbeki can be seen as a "man of action" in Friedrich Nietzche's sense and as a producer of Nietzchean antiquarian history in connection with his call for an African renaissance. According to Nietzsche, antiquarian history is a non-factual type of history that serves life partly by being a kind of "opium" that—like religion in Marx's account—satisfies and pacifies the people; unlike Marx, however, Nietzsche is of the view that the opium effect is positive. Mbeki has argued that there is a moral vacuum in post-apartheid South Africa, and he has presented *ubuntu* as something to be used politically to transform society. In fact, Mbeki has stated that: "Indeed the work we have done in pursuit of the vision and principles of our liberation has all the time been based on the age-old values of *ubuntu*."[24]

The book ends with a discussion of Mogobe Ramose's and Van Binsbergen's debate on *ubuntu*. In Ramose's view, *ubuntu* was the value-orientation of precolonial Southern African villages. He believes that it is authentically rendered in contemporary academic statements of *ubuntu* philosophy. Van Binsbergen claims, on the other hand, that rather than this, *ubuntu* is a contemporary academic and political construct. In my view, Ramose's and Van Binsbergen's positions on *ubuntu* represent a Scylla and a Charybdis and I therefore argue for a middle position that sails between them.[25] The problem with Van Binsbergen's position is that he recognizes neither the deep historical roots of the word *ubuntu*, nor that some contemporary interpretations of *ubuntu* are historical. The weakness of Ramose's position, on the other hand, is that it seems to ignore *ubuntu's* instrumentalist dimensions. These dimensions are highlighted by Van Binsbergen, who, inspired by John L. Austin's distinction between different kinds of speech acts,[26] argues that many *ubuntu* statements have a perlocutionary nature because they aim to persuade or convince. I believe he is right in this regard. For example, Mbeki's antiquarian *ubuntu* history is perlocutionary in nature; it is first and foremost intended to persuade South Africans to buy into the political *ubuntu* ideology that he presents.

The political use of *ubuntu* in South Africa cannot be understood in isolation. Thus in chapter two, I will demonstrate that the post-apartheid call for a return to *ubuntu* echoes a call for Africanization that has also figured prominently in previous postcolonial African transition periods, where narratives of return have also been used politically.

NOTES

1. Antjie Krog, "'This Thing Called Reconciliation . . . ' Forgiveness as Part of an Interconnectedness-Towards-Wholeness," *South African Journal of Philosophy* 27, no. 4 (2008): 354.

2. I have travelled around most of South Africa to conduct qualitative interviews about *ubuntu* and the TRC. A first round of interviews was made in 2008, and a second in 2009. My interviewees include apartheid victims, former commissioners and committee members of the TRC, traditional leaders, conflict resolution practitioners, politicians, and academics. I have received permissions to use the specific quotes that are included in this book, and also to use my interviewees' real names.

3. In ethnophilosophy, African philosophy is characterized as a property belonging to a group, rather than ascribed to a particular individual. Some ethnophilosophical texts focus on specific ethnic groups, others on clusters of related ethnic groups, or even on Africans in general. As will be unfolded later, Placide Tempels' *Bantu Philosophy* is a famous example of an ethnophilosophical text. In this book, Tempels sets out to describe the philosophy of the Bantu peoples (see note 20 below). He claims that the philosophy is shared by all the Bantu, and that it is static: "Their philosophical and ontological conceptions, so far as they are applicable to being in itself have, for the Bantu, absolute and necessary validity, admitting no exception. It would, therefore, be fundamentally erroneous to suggest that the conceptions and principles of the Bantu are essentially variable, uncertain and arbitrary." Placide Tempels, *Bantu Philosophy*, trans. Colin King (Paris: Présence Africaine, 1959), 55.

4. Constitution of the Republic of South Africa, Act 200 of 1993, Epilogue after Section 251, http://www.justice.gov.za/trc/legal/sacon93.htm.

5. Azanian Peoples Organization and Others v. The President of South Africa and Others, No. CCT 17/96 (Constitutional Court of South Africa, Decided July 25, 1996), §19, http://www.justice.gov.za/trc/legal/azapo.htm.

6. The State v. T. Makwanyane and M. Mchunu, No. CCT/3/94 (Constitutional Court of South Africa, Delivered June 6, 1995), §237, http://www.constitutionalcourt.org.za/Archimages/2353.PDF.

7. Port Elisabeth Municipality v. Various Occupiers, No. CCT 53/03 (Constitutional Court of South Africa, Decided Oct. 1, 2004), § 37, http://www.constitutionalcourt.org.za/Archimages/15106.PDF.

8. D. Dikoko v. T. Z. Mokhatla, No. CCT 62/05 (Constitutional Court of South Africa, Decided Aug. 3, 2006), § 113, http://www.constitutionalcourt.org.za/Archimages/7541.PDF.

9. *Makwanyane and Mchunu*, §227.

10. Kwasi Wiredu, "Social Philosophy in Postcolonial Africa: Some Preliminaries Concerning Communalism and Communitarianism," *South African Journal of Philosophy* 27, no. 4 (2008): 332.

11. Leonhard Praeg, *African Philosophy and the Quest for Autonomy: A Philosophical Investigation* (Amsterdam: Editions Rodopi, 2000), 63–130.

12. UN Secretary General, *The Rule of Law and Transitional Justice in Conflict and Post-Conflict Societies*, UN Doc. S/2004/616, Aug. 23, 2004, § 8.

13. Priscilla B. Hayner, *Unspeakable Truths: Transitional Justice and the Challenge of Truth Commissions*, 2nd ed. (New York and London: Routledge, 2011).

14. The TRC followed the Norgaard principles regarding proportionality and political motivation. See Lyn S. Graybill, *Truth and Reconciliation in South Africa: Miracle or Model?* (Boulder and London: Lynne Rienner Publishers, 2002), 70.

15. For further information about the TRC, see: Promotion of National Unity and Reconciliation, Act 34 of 1995 (1995), http://www.justice.gov.za/legislation/acts/1995-034.pdf; *Truth and Reconciliation Commission of South Africa Report*, vol. 1–5 (Cape Town: Truth and Reconciliation Commission, 1998), http://www.justice.gov.za/trc/report/; *Truth and Reconciliation Commission of South Africa Report*, vol. 6–7 (Cape Town: Truth and Reconciliation Commission, 2003), http://www.justice.gov.za/trc/report/.

16. In this connection, see Deborah Posel, "The TRC Report: What Kind of History? What Kind of Truth?" (paper presented at the conference "The TRC: Commissioning the Past," University of Witwatersrand, 1999).

17. Richard A. Wilson, *The Politics of Truth and Reconciliation in South Africa: Legitimizing the Post-Apartheid State* (Cambridge: Cambridge University Press, 2001), 13.

18. Glenda Wildschut, interviewed by author, Oct. 27, 2008, Cape Town.

19. See Henry Odera Oruka, *Trends in Contemporary African Philosophy* (Nairobi: Shirikon Publishers, 1990); Frederick Ochieng'-Odhiambo, *Trends and Issues in African Philosophy* (New York: Peter Lang, 2010).

20. The Bantu are the indigenous Bantu-speaking African peoples. As explained by Derek Nurse, Bantu is the largest of the dozen or so language families that make up

the Niger-Congo phylum, which, with nearly 1500 languages, is the largest phylum in the world. Some 750 million people live in Africa, some 400 million speak a Niger-Congo language, and some 250 million—a third of all Africans—speak a Bantu language. Bantu-speaking communities live south of a line from western Cameroon across the Central African Republic, the Democratic Republic of Congo (DRC; once known as Zaire), Uganda, and northern Kenya to southern Somalia. Most languages spoken from that line to the southern tip of South Africa are Bantu. See Derek Nurse, "Bantu Languages," in *Encyclopedia of Language and Linguistics*, ed. Keith Brown, 2nd ed. (New York: Elsevier, 2006), 679.

21. Tempels, *Bantu Philosophy*, 50.

22. I am not the first to use such approaches in relation to African philosophy. Michael Onyebuchi Eze, for example, has also been looking into the historical dimensions of African philosophy, including historical dimensions of *ubuntu*. See Eze, *Intellectual History in Contemporary South Africa*.

23. Wim van Binsbergen, "*Ubuntu* and the Globalization of Southern African Thought and Society," *Quest* 15, no. 1–2 (2001): 82.

24. Thabo Mbeki, "Resignation Speech" (address to the people by the South African president, Sep. 21, 2008).

25. Scylla and Charybdis are two dangerous sea monsters that Odysseus and his crew have to sail between while traversing a treacherous and narrow channel in book twelve of Homer's *Odyssey*.

26. See John L. Austin, *How to Do Things With Words* (Oxford: Oxford University Press, 1962).

TWO
African Philosophy for Change[1]

There has been an intimate relationship between African philosophy and societal change. During the early years of decolonization, a number of African political leaders identified traditional African socialist and nationalist philosophies as important resources for positive change and development in society. By looking to such philosophies as sources of societal guidance, African leaders attempted to reconstruct society from an African standpoint. They sought to reaffirm the dignity and autonomy of Africans by underscoring that the new postcolonial societies, rather than being built on the ideas of their former colonial oppressors, should be founded on positive ideas and values from their own African cultures. In an article about social philosophy in postcolonial Africa, Wiredu explains that:

> The leaders in question [Kwame Nkrumah (Ghana), Léopold Senghor (Senegal), Julius Nyerere (Tanzania), Obafemi Awolowo (Nigeria), Kenneth Kaunda (Zambia) and Ahmed Sékou Touré (Guinea)] had an equally strong sense of the importance of cultural self-identity. Colonialism had in varying degrees scored African culture. Now after independence they needed to reassert their own culture, and not just cosmetically. National reconstruction is a cultural enterprise of the highest kind. At independence the easy option was to stick by the systems in which the colonial powers left us. These were copies, imperfect copies, to be sure, of what were in place in the colonialist countries. These leaders did not go for that easy option. They understood that the colonial systems needed to be reviewed from an African standpoint.[2]

Chapter 2
NARRATIVES OF RETURN IN POSTCOLONIAL AFRICA

Some of the narratives that were recounted to restore African dignity in the former colonies that gained their independence in the late 1950s and 1960s can be characterized as narratives of return because they contain the idea that a return to something African is necessary in order for society to prosper.[3] I want to share two general observations about these narratives. The first is that narratives of return have often been constructed and discussed in the context of societal transformations in which political leaders, academics, and others have attempted to identify past values that they believed should inspire politics and life in general in the future society. The second observation is that African postcolonial narratives of return have typically contained the idea that in order to create a good future, society needs to return to something African which, rather than originating in the previous period of colonial oppression, is rooted in precolonial times.

Broadly speaking, the postcolonial African narratives of return thus tend to divide history into three phases: first, the precolonial phase which, often but not always, is perceived as a "golden age" characterized by harmony; second, a period of decline, which is understood to have been brought about by intruders who attempted to deprive the Africans of their resources, dignity, and culture; and third, a phase of recovery in which Africans, having gained sufficient political power, attempt to restore their dignity and culture by returning to (what are claimed to be) traditional philosophical ideas and values.

Julius Nyerere's ideas about *ujamaa* provide a good example of an early postcolonial narrative of return. Nyerere was sworn in as president of the newly independent Republic of Tanganyika in December 1962. In April 1964, he became president of the new United Republic of Tanganyika and Zanzibar, in October 1964 renamed the United Republic of Tanzania. He continued as president until his retirement in 1985. In the introduction to *Freedom and Socialism* (1968), he explains that across almost all of Africa, "the first and most vocal demand of the people after independence was for Africanization."[4] Nyerere supported the call for Africanization and argued that in Tanganyika, and later also in Tanzania, Africanization should take the form of a return to *ujamaa*, which he described as a traditional African form of socialism. In the same text, he also explains why he thinks Africanization necessary:

> Years of Arab slave raiding, and later years of European domination, had caused our people to have grave doubt about their own abilities. This was no accident; any dominating group seeks to destroy the confidence of those they dominate because this helps them to maintain their position, and the oppressors in Tanganyika were no exception.[5]

Nyerere was convinced that after independence a new historical phase of recovery had begun in Tanganyika. He described this phase of recovery as a revolution: "It is a revolution with a purpose, and that purpose is the extension to all African citizens of the requirements on human dignity."[6] Furthermore, he argued that the revolution could fulfill its purpose if society returned to its traditional socialism. This traditional socialism was to be reinvented as *ujamaa* (a Swahili word meaning "familyhood"), which, for Nyerere, represented a unique African kind of socialism that differed significantly from the European version:

> European socialism was born of the Agrarian Revolution and the Industrial Revolution which followed it. The former created the "landed" and the "landless" classes in society; the later produced the modern capitalist and the industrial proletariat. These two revolutions planted the seeds of conflict within society, and not only was European socialism born of that conflict, but its apostles sanctified the conflict into a philosophy. Civil war was no longer looked upon as something evil, or something unfortunate, but as something good and necessary. As prayer is to Christianity or to Islam, so civil war (which they called "class war") is to the European version of socialism—a means inseparable from the end.[7]

According to Nyerere, the true African socialist does not consider one class of men as his brethren and another as his enemies. He or she does not form an alliance with the "brethren" for the extermination of the "non-brethren;" rather, they regard all human beings as members of an extended family. The African socialism of *ujamaa* is therefore founded not on class struggle, but on the harmony of the extended family. Nyerere has explained that:

> *Ujamaa*, then, or "familyhood," describes our socialism. It is opposed to capitalism, which seeks to build a happy society on the basis of the exploitation of man by man; and it is equally opposed to doctrinaire socialism which seeks to build its happy society on a philosophy of inevitable conflict between man and man. We, in Africa, have no more need of being "converted" to socialism than we have of being "taught" democracy. Both are rooted in our own past—in the traditional society which produced us.[8]

Narratives of return also developed in other African countries that became independent in the late 1950s and 1960s. After independence in Ghana in 1957, President Kwame Nkrumah argued that politics should be inspired by the philosophy of *consciencism*, which he held to be in harmony with the original humanist principles of Africa.[9] He believed that the former colonial administrators of Ghana, along with those of their African employees who "became infected with European ideals,"[10] had abandoned these humanist principles. Another example is postcolonial Senegal, where President Léopold Senghor argued that Senegalese socialism should be inspired by *négritude*, which he identified as the totality of traditional civilizing values of the negro world.[11] There are therefore many variations on the narratives of return. Furthermore, the consequences of the return are highly contested, as explained by Mabogo P. More in his article "African Renaissance: The Politics of Return."[12] While some scholars perceive the return as a revival of the peaceful golden age of Rousseau's "noble savage," others perceive it as a return to a Hobbesian state of nature where the life of man is "solitary, poore, nasty, brutish and short."[13]

UBUNTU AND THE CREATION OF ZIMBABWE

Some of the narratives which have developed about *ubuntu* in post-apartheid South Africa are also narratives of return, and they share a number of characteristics with the narratives of return presented during the early years of decolonization. *Ubuntu*, however, was used in the political process prior to the South African transition process, namely in the context of the creation of Zimbabwe.

As already mentioned in chapter one, there are many old written sources on *ubuntu*. The first book to be published specifically on *ubuntu*, however, was *Hunhuism or Ubuntuism: A Zimbabwe Indigenous Political Philosophy* (1980). This book was written by Stanlake Samkange, a Zimbabwean historian and nationalist politician, and his wife Tommie Marie Samkange, an American psychologist. The Samkanges explain that:

> the attention one human being gives to another: the kindness, courtesy, consideration and friendliness in the relationship between people; a code of behavior, an attitude to other people and to life, is embodied in *hunhu* or *ubuntu* [the Samkange use the Shona word *hunhu* and the Nguni word *ubuntu* as pseudonyms].[14]

Furthermore, they argue that *ubuntu* is connected to a political philosophy or ideology, and they explicitly put this idea forward within the social context of the transition from white minority rule to black majority rule in the new Zimbabwe, asking: "Is there a philosophy or ideology indigenous to the country that can serve its people just as well, if not better than, foreign ideologies?"[15] With regard to this question, they explain:

> It is the thesis of this book that Zimbabwe has an indigenous political philosophy which can best guide and inspire thinking in this new era of Zimbabwe. This philosophy or ideology, *the authors endeavor to show* [emphasis mine], exists and can best be described as Hunhuism or Ubuntuism.[16]

Thus the Samkanges present the notion that there exists a philosophy or ideology indigenous to Zimbabwe as a *hypothesis*, with the implication that this is not self-evident to all. Stanlake Samkange even relates how at the Geneva constitutional talks he told some students that he was a "Hunhuist." It turned out that they did not know about Hunhuism, and he said:

> "Whose fault is it," I asked, "if no one knows about the philosophy of your grandfather and mine? Is it not your fault and mine? We are the intellectuals of Zimbabwe. It is our business to distill this philosophy and set it out for the whole world to see."[17]

Accordingly, the Samkanges set out to distill the indigenous philosophy of Hunhuism or Ubuntuism. They appear to identify Hunhuism or Ubuntuism as a philosophy about how the new Zimbabwe should be influenced by *ubuntu*, understood as a human quality. As mentioned in the introduction, this understanding of *ubuntu* has deep historical roots. Furthermore, the Samkanges describe Hunhuism or Ubuntuism first and foremost as a *political* philosophy, reflected in the fact that eleven of the book's seventeen chapters (chapters six to sixteen) are dedicated to a description of how policy should be formulated in the new Zimbabwe in order to be consistent with this philosophy. Some of the political implications that they extracted from Hunhuism or Ubuntuism were the following:

1. Hunhuism or Ubuntuism indicates that there should be a governance of national unity in the new Zimbabwe (see page 45).[18]
2. According to Hunhuism or Ubuntuism, the new Zimbabweans set out to live amicably with their neighboring states (see page 50).
3. To be consistent with Hunhuism or Ubuntuism, the new Zimbabwean government should use the inhabitants' fear of *ngozi* (aggrieved spirits) to discourage murder (see page 54).
4. Hunhuism or Ubuntuism does not allow that the African idea of communal land ownership be eroded by Western ideas of private land ownership (see page 59).
5. According to Hunhuism or Ubuntuism, there should be state, communal and individual property (see page 64).

By connecting *ubuntu* with the *political* philosophy of Hunhuism or Ubuntuism, the Samkanges grafted political connotations onto the word *ubuntu*. Nevertheless, despite this politicizing interpretation, Hunhuism or Ubuntuism did not markedly influence politics in the new Zimbabwe. For example, I have been unable to find any Zimbabwean legal documents that mention Hunhuism or Ubuntuism, and a search for this philosophy on the website of the Zimbabwean government failed to produce any references.[19] Nevertheless, some have celebrated Robert Mugabe for displaying *ubuntu* politically,[20] and Mugabe has used the term *ubuntu* himself. In a newspaper article entitled "Zimbabwe Celebrates Peace

Days," published in the *Zimbabwe Telegraph* on June 24, 2009, it was reported that:

> Zimbabwean President Robert Mugabe has last week proclaimed Friday, Saturday and Sunday as peace days—during which Zimbabweans from different political persuasions are expected to encourage and promote national healing and reconciliation. Mugabe said the three days set aside for national healing offered Zimbabweans a choice to either consolidate their identity or expose themselves as a disintegrated nation. "We should realize that the desire for peace, harmony and stability is a desire for progress, national identity, prosperity and *hunhu, ubuntu*," he said.[21]

UBUNTU AND THE SOUTH AFRICAN TRANSITION TO DEMOCRACY

According to Hannah Arendt, rather than itself being a manifestation of power, violence often emerges when power is challenged.[22] When the power of the South African apartheid regime was put under pressure by the black majority population, the regime substituted power with violence. The first major example of this was the Sharpeville massacre on March 21, 1960, when sixty-nine people were killed when the police opened fire on a crowd that demonstrated peacefully against the racist pass laws. The massacre was followed by strikes, the declaration of a state of emergency, and the banning of both the African National Congress (ANC) and the Pan Africanist Congress (PAC). Subsequently, these two organizations, together with other political organizations, abandoned their nonviolent strategies against apartheid for violent ones.

The armed struggle against apartheid, combined with international sanctions, finally led the apartheid government to set up secret meetings with Mandela from 1985.[23] Later, on February 2, 1990, President Frederik Willem de Klerk lifted the bans on the ANC, the PAC, and other political organizations. He also declared that Mandela would be released from prison, and this duly took place on February 11, 1990. The following multi-party negotiation process led to the ratification of the interim constitution on November 18, 1993, and to South Africa's first democratic election on April 27, 1994.[24] With the ANC gaining just under 63 percent of the votes, Mandela became president and de Klerk and Mbeki deputies.

The interim constitution was intended to provide "a historic bridge between the past of a deeply divided society characterized by strife, conflict, untold suffering and injustice, and a future founded on the recognition of human rights, democracy and peaceful coexistence and development opportunities for all South Africans, irrespective of color, race, class, belief or sex."[25] The quotation is taken from the epilogue of the interim constitution, which defined the nature of the chosen "bridge" away from apartheid by stating that in addressing the divisions and strife of the past, "there is a need for understanding but not for vengeance, a need for reparation but not for retaliation, a need for *ubuntu* but not for victimization."[26] According to the South African Constitutional Court, the appearance of the word *ubuntu* in the epilogue was neither coincidental nor unimportant. This is well illustrated by the quotes from the Court cited in chapter one.

Nevertheless, despite the importance ascribed to *ubuntu* by the Constitutional Court, the Court has not explained in detail how the word came to be included in the epilogue. The Court has stated that those who negotiated the interim constitution made a deliberate choice to prefer understanding, reparation, and *ubuntu* over vengeance, retaliation, and victimization.[27] But this is broad-brush information. It would be interesting to know the details of how the word *ubuntu* came to be incorporated. Who suggested that the word should be included? Did the negotiators discuss whether it should be included or not? And if so, exactly how did the discussion develop? I have been unable to find any texts that answer these questions. Mfuniselwa John Bhengu, a former member of Parliament for Inkatha Freedom Party (IFP) and an acknowledged author on *ubuntu*, has informed me that:

> I really don't know who came up with it [the word *ubuntu* in the epilogue]. All that I know is that during Codesa [Conversation for a Democratic South Africa] negotiations at Kempton Park in 1993, there were many African leaders who participated, and it could be that *ubuntu* as a spark came up during the negotiations or among those who were writing the constitution. The IFP was one of the negotiators at Codesa, and I am sure that, even if it didn't come from it, they [IFP] supported such move.[28]

To support my research, Bhengu has conducted inquiries among South African members of parliament about who may be aware of how the term *ubuntu* came to be included in the epilogue, unfortunately with no luck: "I have tried to ask some of them who were there [during the negotiations of the interim constitution] but they cannot remember how it came about."[29] Considering that the epilogue is a very important and sensitive text in the interim constitution, I find it surprising that no one appears to have a clear recollection of how the word *ubuntu* came to be included.

The epilogue is important and sensitive because it contains the negotiated agreement about how the divisions and strife of the apartheid era are to be dealt with in the new democratic South Africa. Immediately after the statement that "there is a need for understanding but not for vengeance, a need for reparation but not for retaliation, a need for *ubuntu* but not for victimization," the epilogue explains that: "In order to advance such reconciliation and reconstruction, amnesty shall be granted in respect of acts, omissions and offenses associated with political objectives and committed in the course of the conflicts of the past."[30] In the next sentence, the epilogue decrees that the parliament should adopt a law to establish the mechanisms, criteria, and procedures by which amnesty should be dealt with. This was done with the Promotion of National Unity and Reconciliation Act, which established the South African TRC. The TRC has been briefly discussed in chapter one. In chapter three, I will move on to contextualize the TRC within the landscape of transitional justice.

NOTES

1. This chapter includes material from my article: Christian B. N. Gade, "The Historical Development of the Written Discourses on Ubuntu," *South African Journal of Philosophy* 30, no. 3 (2011): 303–29.

2. Wiredu, "Social Philosophy in Postcolonial Africa," 332.

3. As mentioned in the introduction, my use of the phrase "narratives of return" is inspired by Praeg's book *African Philosophy and the Quest for Autonomy*.

4. Julius Nyerere, *Freedom and Socialism* (Oxford: Oxford University Press, 1968), 27.

5. Julius Nyerere, *Freedom and Unity* (Oxford: Oxford University Press, 1996), 3.

6. Ibid., 22.

7. Ibid., 169.

8. Ibid., 170.

9. Kwame Nkrumah, *Consciencism* (London: Heinemann, 1964), 70.

10. Ibid., 69.

11. Léopold Senghor, *Pierre Teilhard de Chardin et la politique africaine* (Paris: Editions du Seuil, 1962), 20.

12. Mabogo P. More, "African Renaissance: The Politics of Return," *African Journal of Political Science* 7, no. 2 (2002).

13. Thomas Hobbes, *Leviathan* (New York: W. W. Norton & Company, 1997), 70.

14. Stanlake Samkange and Tommie Marie Samkange, *Hunhuism or Ubuntuism: A Zimbabwe Indigenous Political Philosophy* (Salisbury: Graham Publishing, 1980), 39.

15. Ibid., page inside the front page.

16. Ibid.

17. Ibid., 9.

18. More specifically, they call for "a Government of National Unity in which all political parties represented in Parliament will participate so that, with malice towards none and charity for all, we can all, with dignity, set about rebuilding and healing the wounds we have inflicted on ourselves." Ibid., 45.

19. The website of the Zimbabwean government can be found on http://www.gta.gov.zw/. The Southern African Legal Information Institute (SAFLII) provides access to Zimbabwean legal documents (see http://www.saflii.org).

20. See Desmond Tutu, *No Future Without Forgiveness* (London: Rider, 1999), 36; Mfuniselwa J. Bhengu, *Ubuntu: The Essence of Democracy* (Cape Town: Novalis Press, 1996), 29.

21. In June 2009, the article was available at http://www.zimtelegraph.com/?p=1816.

22. She writes: "Power and violence are opposites; where the one rules absolutely, the other is absent. Violence appears where power is in jeopardy, but left to its own course it ends in power's disappearance." Hannah Arendt, *On Violence* (San Diego: Harvest Book, 1970), 56.

23. See Nelson Mandela, *Long Walk to Freedom* (London: Abacus, 1994), 609 ff. A good overview of the armed apartheid conflict is presented in *TRC Report*, vol. 2, chap.

1. For an overview of sanctions against the apartheid state, see Philip I. Levy, "Sanctions on South Africa: What Did They Do?" (Center Discussion Paper No. 796, Economic Growth Center, Yale University, New Haven, Connecticut, Feb., 1999).

24. The interim constitution was a transitional constitution: "One of its principal purposes was to set out the procedures for the negotiation and drafting of a 'final' Constitution. Once the final Constitution was adopted, the interim Constitution fell away. But in spite of its transitional status, the interim Constitution was binding, supreme and fully justiciable." C. G. van der Merwe and Jacques E. du Plessis, *Introduction to the Law of South Africa* (The Hague: Kluwer Law International, 2004), 63. The final constitution was adopted on May 8, 1996. Unlike the interim constitution, the constitution of 1996 does not contain the word *ubuntu* (see Constitution of the Republic of South Africa, Act 108 of 1996).

25. Constitution of the Republic of South Africa, Act 200 of 1993, Epilogue after Section 251.

26. Ibid.

27. Azanian Peoples Organization and Others v. The President of South Africa and Others, No. CCT 17/96 (Constitutional Court of South Africa, Decided July 25, 1996), §19, http://www.justice.gov.za/trc/legal/azapo.htm.

28. Mufuniselwa John Bhengu, e-mail to author, Dec. 20, 2009. It should be noted that according to the preamble of the Constitution of Inkatha Freedom Party (1996), the IFP embraces the principles of *ubuntu*. Michael Onyebuchi Eze writes that: "While *no love was lost* between the ANC government and Inkatha prior to the draft Constitution [the interim constitution], a possible hypothesis could be that the insertion of *ubuntu/botho* in the preamble to the draft Constitution was a possible influence or adaptation from Inkatha's Constitution. One could imagine if the eventual deletion of *ubuntu* from the final Constitution constitutes a further attempt by the ANC led government to distance itself from Inkatha. These are merely factious hypotheses and speculations considering the adaptation of *ubuntu* as a national discourse in the overall process of reconciliation and nation building in South Africa." Eze, *Intellectual History in Contemporary South Africa*, 103.

29. Mufuniselwa John Bhengu, e-mail to author, Jan. 29, 2010.

30. Constitution of the Republic of South Africa, Act No. 200 of 1993, Epilogue after Section 251, http://www.justice.gov.za/trc/legal/sacon93.htm.

THREE
Transitional Justice in South Africa

Rutu Teitel claims to have coined the expression "transitional justice" in 1991.[1] Though her claim is reproduced by several scholars without questioning,[2] it is incorrect, as the expression is found in older texts.[3] It was, however, in the post-1990 period that transitional justice began to develop into a specific research area with specialized transitional justice centers, such as the International Center for Transitional Justice, and journals such as the *International Journal of Transitional Justice*. In recent years, transitional justice has been the subject of immense interest, leading to the current situation in which transitional justice has become a buzzword, defined and used in various different senses.[4] Former UN Secretary General Kofi Annan for example describes transitional justice in the following way:

> The notion of "transitional justice" discussed in the present report comprises the full range of processes and mechanisms associated with a society's attempts to come to terms with a legacy of large-scale past abuses, in order to ensure accountability, serve justice, and achieve reconciliation. These mechanisms may include both judicial and non-judicial mechanisms, with differing levels of international involvement (or not at all) and individual prosecutions, reparations, truth-seeking, institutional reform, vetting and dismissals, or a combination thereof.[5]

The history of transitional justice mechanisms has been presented in several different ways. Teitel begins her famous genealogy of transitional justice with the Nuremberg trials after World War II,[6] while Jon Elster points out that the kind of mechanisms that are labeled as "transitional justice" have a long history that can be traced all the way back to antiquity. He highlights that in classical Greece, Athens had two episodes of transitional justice: first after the demise of the oligarchy in 411 BC, and then later in 403 BC after the overthrow of the second oligarchy. Elster explains that in the first transition period, the Athenians who restored the pre-oligarchic democracy carried out harsh retribution, while they reacted differently in the second period as they pulled their punches in dealing with the oligarchs, preferring the forward-looking goal of social reconciliation over the backwards-looking goal of retribution.[7]

DEALING WITH VIOLATIONS OF THE PAST

It has often been pointed out that transitional justice is about "dealing with the past." In fact, this phrase has developed into a kind of transitional justice mantra. In one sense, as human beings, we are constantly dealing with our past. We live in a "field of tension" between the past, the present, and the future, and the way we think and behave at present is often influenced by our past (or—which is important in the context of this book—our ideas and narratives about the past) and by the expectations, hopes, fears, etc., that we hold for the future. Transitional justice, however, is not about dealing with the past in an everyday sense. In Shashi Tharoor's *Riot*, one of the characters says:

> I'll tell you what your problem is in India. You have too much history. Far more than you can use peacefully. So you end up wielding history like a battle axe, against each other.[8]

The social context of transitional justice is precisely a context with "too much history": a context where history risks becoming a "battle axe" because it contains severe violations that continue to haunt people in the present. There are multiple and conflicting views on how to handle such contexts in the best manner. Tutu has frequently pointed out that forgetting the past is not an option, and that the violations of the past have to be remembered if similar violations are to be avoided in the future. In a conversation with the historian John Hope Franklin, he says:

> We might think that we have control over our memories, and that we have shut them out, but they have this uncanny habit of being able to return and haunt us. I remember, fairly recently, visiting Dachau, the former concentration camp [in Germany], and there they have established a museum, and they have Santayana's haunting words written over the top [. . .] "Those who forget the past are doomed to repeat it" [. . .] In South Africa, you have people say: "Let bygones be bygones," and you say: "Unfortunately, they don't become bygones just because, by fiat, you declare them to be so." And I think, I mean, that we, we need to do all we can to help our children appropriate their history, appropriate the memory.[9]

However, not everyone agrees with Tutu that the past has to be remembered. As will be unfolded in chapter seven, Nietzsche argues that we should create stories about the past that serve life in the present, rather than attempting to remember the past as it really was. In Nietzsche's view, an obsession with truth hurts the living, and I cannot but wonder whether he could be right. The idea that we must deal with the past by truth-seeking or other transitional justice mechanisms could be problematic in some contexts. In this connection, it is worth pointing to a democratization process like that in Spain after the end of the dictatorship of Francisco Franco. In the years following the transition, there was no transitional justice but rather an attempt to let bygones be bygones, and Spain still developed into a well-functioning democracy.

The specific types of abuse dealt with by means of transitional justice have differed from country to country, ranging from the Holocaust to the disappearances under the Argentinian and Chilean military dictatorships of the 1970s and 1980s, ethnic cleansing in the former Yugoslavia in the 1990s and the genocide in Rwanda of 1994, to mention but a few examples. In South Africa, the TRC was tasked with establishing as complete a picture as possible of the causes, nature, and extent of gross human rights violations committed between March 1, 1960, and May 10, 1994. In the Promotion of National Unity and Reconciliation Act, gross violations of human rights were defined as killing, abduction, torture, and severe ill-treatment. Thus the truth-seeking mission of the TRC was focused on direct violence, while structural and cultural violence received less attention.

Johan Galtung explains that in direct violence an actor commits the violence, while structural violence is built into social and economic structures and shows up as unequal power and thus as unequal life chances.[10] Cultural violence is those aspects of culture—for example ideological or religious ideas—that can be used to justify or legitimize direct or structural violence.[11] During apartheid, structural violence was omnipresent, as the apartheid laws introduced societal structures that discriminated against the non-white majority of the population in almost all spheres of life. Cultural violence was also widespread, for instance in form of the social Darwinist idea that the South African population was composed of different races which should develop separately because they were at different levels of development, or certain varieties of Calvinist ideas according to which whites are predestined to rule over blacks. The TRC process has been criticized for not paying sufficient attention to such structural and cultural forms of violence, thereby painting a flawed picture of apartheid that neglects the systemic dimension of the violations that were committed. As Christoph Marx writes:

> By remembering selectively the monstrosities, and by leaving out the everyday activities of white employers, the pettiness of the "madams," or the permanent terror of the pass laws, any public discussion of apartheid as a system is circumvented. The one-sidedness of forgiving without any adequate response in the form of regret can be explained through this separation of physical violence from the repressive struc-

tures that carried it out. It is like the call into an empty room—the addressees, the former supporters of apartheid, do not feel addressed. There is reason to fear that by separating the worst terrorist atrocities from the repressive structures within which they were committed, the necessary lessons for the future will not be established.[12]

Furthermore, although the TRC did an immense job in uncovering the truth about gross human rights violations, it presented only a partial history of these violations. Of course, this had to do with the fact that it was impossible for a commission with limited resources to uncover all violations that had been perpetrated, but it also had to do with the fact that the TRC selected specific stories for its public hearings.[13] Ilan Lax, who was a member of both the Human Rights Violations Committee and the Amnesty Committee, has told me that:

> I can remember many times sitting in [TRC] meetings with two hundred files on the table. We now had to go to some place in the country, unpacking all the different kinds of cases, and we would put together a matrix: Who were the parties involved? Over what time frame? Over what geographical spread? What are the kinds of things that happened? What are the stories that we could allow to be told? Which stories should we be choosing that would reflect the experience of people, so that they would be able to say: "Yes, that is what happened in my village! Yes, that is what happened in my township!" and therefore feel acknowledged and vindicated?—this idea of vicarious catharsis or vicarious acknowledgment.[14]

In fact, as already mentioned in chapter one, only about 10 percent of the 21,290 people who testified to the Human Rights Violations Committee got a chance to tell their stories in public victim hearings. The transcripts of the public hearings are available on the TRC website, but the public does not have access to the remaining 90 percent of testimonies. So even though the TRC places a lot of emphasis on truth, the truth that the public received was a partial one.

RETRIBUTIVE AND RESTORATIVE JUSTICE

The truth about the past plays different roles in different contexts of transitional justice. In criminal prosecutions such as those of Nuremberg and Tokyo after World War II, the main aim of truth-seeking was to establish guilt. In those contexts, truth-seeking was related to retributive justice, where justice is considered to consist in proportionality between crime and punishment. It has often been argued that the TRC was linked to another kind of justice, namely restorative justice. Ann Skelton and Cheryl Frank refer for example to the TRC as "South Africa's most famous and engaging experience with restorative justice,"[15] and according to Alex Boraine, the vice chairman of the TRC, "[r]estorative justice has manifested itself in the concept of a truth commission and in the South African model in particular."[16] Tutu also connects the TRC with restorative justice, and he associates this kind of justice with *ubuntu*:

> [Restorative justice] was characteristic of traditional African jurisprudence. Here the central concern is not retribution or punishment but, in the spirit of *ubuntu*, the healing of breaches, the redressing of imbalances, the restoration of broken relationships.[17]

Like Tutu, Richard Bell connects restorative justice and *ubuntu*, and he states that: "It is in the correlation between *ubuntu*, rooted in whatever forms of 'communalism' may survive in South Africa (moderate or otherwise), and the kind of justice referred to as 'restorative justice,' that we find the foundation stones for the Truth and Reconciliation Commission and a possibility for a moral and spiritual renaissance."[18] This idea of an intimate connection between the TRC, restorative justice and *ubuntu* is also presented in the section of the TRC Report entitled "*Ubuntu*: Promoting Restorative Justice," but there it is pointed out that the TRC may not fully meet the ideals of restorative justice. According to the report, restorative justice demands that perpetrators contribute to the restoration of the well-being of their victims. Thus,

> The fact that people were given their freedom without taking responsibility for some form of restitution remains a major problem with the amnesty process. Only if the emerging truth releases a social dynamics that includes redressing the suffering of victims will it meet the ideal of restorative justice.[19]

However, some perpetrators did offer restitution after receiving amnesty, as illustrated by the story of Brian Mitchell. After Mitchell was granted amnesty for his role in killing eleven people in the 1988 Trust Feed Massacre, Khoza Mgojo, one of the TRC commissioners, led a group that set up a meeting in Trust Feed between Mitchell and the people affected by the killings. Mgojo has told me that:

> It was tense! The police had to be there because we did not know what was going to happen. We were just taking the chance. When Brian Mitchell told his story the people were fuming with anger, but at the end of it all the people thanked Brian Mitchell for his courage to come and face them. That is where the relationships started between Brian Mitchell and the community. Mitchell promised that he was going to help them by supporting the community, by raising funds somewhere so that maybe a center for the community could be established. And then the friendship began [which has lasted] up to now. So that is why I say that if people who have done something, if they give back to the people they have injured, it helps—I saw it with Brian Mitchell.[20]

In my view, the relation between the TRC and restorative justice is a highly complex one. The TRC can, as pointed out by several authors, be seen as reflecting restorative justice to a great extent. However, it is noteworthy that restorative justice was not mentioned in the interim constitution, nor in the Promotion of National Unity and Reconciliation Act, which established the TRC. In my article "Restorative Justice and the South African Truth and Reconciliation Process," I argue that the TRC may not have been aware of the notion of restorative justice at the beginning of the TRC process, and that awareness of this notion may have emerged when the South African Law Commission published Issue Paper 7 on restorative justice in April 1997.[21] If this is true, then the TRC Report's description of the TRC as an institution committed to restorative justice represents a retrospective self-interpretation.[22]

SOCIETAL TRANSITIONS AND POWER

Transitional justice is about justice in the context of societal transitions. Different types of transitions result in different power structures in the post-transition societies, and these structures may set limits on the possibilities for transitional justice. The South African transition process after apartheid was one of democratization, more specifically the kind of process described by Huntington as a transplacement in his book *The Third Wave: Democratization in the Late Twentieth Century*. In this book, Huntington distinguishes between transformations, replacements, and transplacements as three main forms of democratic transition, each with differing power consequences.

Transformations are top-down democratization processes initiated by political leaders of the authoritarian regime when they gradually begin to liberalize and introduce reforms. The Chilean transition to democracy is an example. In this transition, Augusto Pinochet ensured a blanket amnesty for himself and other representatives of the former military regime for crimes committed under the junta, and representatives from the former regime continued to have considerable power after the transition. Pinochet even remained commander-in-chief of the army. Clearly, criminal prosecution was not a transitional justice possibility for the new Chilean government, led by President Patricio Aylwin. Instead, Aylwin established a truth commission through presidential decree with a mandate to investigate human rights abuses resulting in death or disappearance under military rule from September 11, 1973, to March 11, 1990. The Commission obtained statements from victims, but there was no involvement of perpetrators.

Replacements are a second major form of democratic transition. Unlike transformations, they are bottom-up transitions, in the sense that it is political opposition groups that take the lead in bringing about democracy by overthrowing the authoritarian government. This means that the former rulers lose power and do not have a say on decisions concerning transitional justice. Some, but not all, replacements are followed by criminal prosecution. For example, after the defeat of the German Nazi regime by the allies at the end of World War II, military trials were set up in Nuremberg; while after the Spanish transition there was no transitional justice at all, but rather—as outlined in chapter one—an attempt to let bygones be bygones.

Transplacements are the final major form of democratization process. As negotiated settlements, they can be characterized as both top-down and bottom-up processes, because they are initiated by actions undertaken jointly by government and opposition groups. After transplacements, the former rulers may still possess considerable power. This was clearly the case after the South African transplacement, where de Klerk, the last apartheid president, became vice president in the ANC-led government. It is unlikely that the former rulers will agree to a political settlement if they risk being prosecuted after the transition to democracy. Thus in South Africa the representatives of the apartheid government would sign the interim constitution only if it included an amnesty clause. This meant that prosecution was not a possibility in South Africa, as also noted by Tutu in the TRC Report:

> There were those who believed that we should follow the post World War II example of putting those guilty of gross violations of human rights on trial as allies did at Nuremberg. In South Africa, where we had a military stalemate, that was clearly an impossible option. Neither side in the struggle (the state nor the liberation movements) had defeated the other and hence nobody was in a position to enforce so-called victor's justice.[23]

TRADITION IN TRANSITIONAL JUSTICE

In transitional justice, as we have seen in this chapter, history is something which is being dealt with in various ways, but also something which "shapes" transitional justice possibilities and impossibilities. History has also been described in this context as a useful resource for the design of transitional justice. In fact, it has frequently been argued that the past contains traditional practices, ideas, and values that ought to inform contemporary transitional justice processes.[24] How "traditional" such practices, ideas, and values are in their modern reformulations may of course vary from case to case, but as Eric Hobsbawm and Terence Rangers remind us in their book *The Invention of Tradition*, traditions that are perceived to be old are sometimes of recent origin.[25]

The South African TRC is an interesting case in relation to the use of history in transitional justice. The idea that the TRC process was founded on traditional *ubuntu* values and thus on the cultural heritage of the majority of the population has—as underscored in chapter one—been interpreted as an attempt to legitimize the TRC. As quoted, Wilson, for example, argues that *ubuntu* became an Africanist "wrapping" used to sell a reconciliatory version of human rights talk to black South Africans. Wilson is definitely correct that there is a political dimension to *ubuntu*, and this dimension will be unpacked in chapter seven. However, as already mentioned in chapter one, he does not pay sufficient attention to the fact that there were only sporadic references to *ubuntu* in the TRC hearings. These references do not constitute a "sales project" of the TRC itself. The selling happened outside the hearings, which I will come back to in the next chapter, where I look into the relationship between the TRC and *ubuntu*.

NOTES

1. Ruti Teitel, "Editorial Note—Transitional Justice Globalized," *The International Journal of Transitional Justice* 2, no. 1 (2008): 1.

2. See, for instance, Padraig McAuliffe, "From Molehills to Mountains (and Myths?): A Critical History of Transitional Justice Advocacy," *Finnish Yearbook of International Law* 22 (2011): 86; Gerald Gahima, *Transitional Justice in Rwanda: Accountability for Atrocity* (London: Routledge, 2013), 1; Alexander Laban Hinton, "Introduction: Towards and Anthropology of Transitional Justice," in *Transitional Justice: Global Mechanisms and Local Realities after Genocide and Mass Violence*, ed. Alexander Laban Hinton (New Brunswick, NJ: Rutgers University Press, 2011), 2.

3. For example, the expression appears in an article from 1947: Arie Poldervaart, "Black-Robed Justice in New Mexico," *New Mexico Historical Review* 22, no. 3 (1947). Here the expression is used to refer to a person who was a justice during a transition period in New Mexico, and thus it had a different meaning than those it has attained in the current transitional justice literature.

4. Several scholars have pointed out that transitional justice has become a buzzword. See for example: Natalia Szablewska and Sascha-Dominik Bachmann, "Introduction," in *Current Issues in Transitional Justice: Towards a More Holistic Approach*, ed. Natalia Szablewska and Sascha-Dominik Bachmann (Heidelberg: Springer, 2015), xi; Gustavo Rojas Paez, "Retaliation in Transitional Justice Scenarios," in *Handbook of Research on Transitional Justice and Peace Building in Turbulent Regions*, ed. Fredy Cante and Hartmut Quehl (Hershey, PA: Information Science Reference), 315.

5. UN Secretary General, *The Rule of Law and Transitional Justice in Conflict and Post-Conflict Societies*, UN Doc. S/2004/616, Aug. 23, 2004, §8.

6. Ruti Teitel, "Transitional Justice Genealogy," *Harvard Human Rights Journal* 16 (2003).

7. Jon Elster, *Closing the Books: Transitional Justice in Historical Perspective* (Cambridge: Cambridge University Press, 2004), 3.

8. Shashi Tharoor, *Riot: A Love Story* (New York: Arcade Publishing, 2001), 205.

9. Quote from the documentary Renée Poussaint, *Tutu and Franklin: A Journey Towards Peace* (Washington, DC: Wisdom Works, 2001).

10. See Johan Galtung, "Violence, Peace, and Peace Research," *Journal of Peace Research* 6, no. 3 (1969): 170–71.

11. See Johan Galtung, "Cultural Violence," *Journal of Peace Research* 27, no. 3 (1990): 291.

12. Christoph Marx, "Ubu and Ubuntu: On the Dialectics of Apartheid and Nation Building," *Politikon* 29, no. 1 (2002): 50.

13. See Deborah Posel, "The TRC Report: What Kind of History? What Kind of Truth?" (paper presented at the conference "The TRC: Commissioning the Past," University of Witwatersrand, 1999).

14. Ilan Lax, interviewed by author, Oct. 24, 2008, Cape Town.

15. Ann Skelton and Cheryl Frank, "Conferencing in South Africa: Returning to Our Future," in *Restorative Justice for Juveniles: Conferencing, Mediation & Circles*, ed. Allison Morris and Gabrielle Maxwell (Oxford: Hart Publishing, 2001), 116.

16. Alex Boraine, *A Country Unmasked: Inside South Africa's Truth and Reconciliation Commission*, (Oxford: Oxford University Press, 2000) 426.

17. Desmond Tutu, *No Future Without Forgiveness* (London: Rider, 1999), 34, 51.

18. Richard Bell, *Understanding African Philosophy: A Cross-Cultural Approach to Classical and Contemporary Issues* (New York: Routledge, 2002), 90.

19. *TRC Report*, vol. 1, 131.

20. Khoza Mgojo, interviewed by author, Nov. 17, 2008, Gamalakhe.

21. Christian B. N. Gade, "Restorative Justice and the South African Truth and Reconciliation Process," *South African Journal of Philosophy* 32, no. 1 (2013): 23.

22. Gade, "Restorative Justice," 24–26.

23. *TRC Report*, vol. 1, 5.

24. See Andrew R. Iliff, "Root and Branch: Discourses on 'Tradition' in Grassroots Transitional Justice," *The International Journal of Transitional Justice* 6, no. 2 (2012); Rosalind Shaw and Lars Waldorf, eds., *Localizing Transitional Justice: Interventions and Priorities after Mass Violence* (Stanford, CA: Stanford University Press, 2010).

25. Eric Hobsbawm and Terence Ranger, eds., *The Invention of Tradition* (Cambridge: Cambridge University Press, 1983).

FOUR
The South African TRC and *Ubuntu*

It has frequently been argued that there is an integral connection between the TRC and *ubuntu*. For example, in the documentary *Truth, Justice, Memory: South Africa's Truth and Reconciliation Process*, Tutu links the TRC and *ubuntu* in an attempt to counter the idea that the TRC undermined justice by offering amnesty to perpetrators:

> I would want to stress still the fact that it [the TRC with its amnesty process] was justice, not retributive justice but restorative justice. We were looking more to heal than to punish the perpetrator. We were looking for a way of dealing with the offenses and the violations in such a way that we were not more disruptive. We were actually using the principles of *ubuntu*, which speaks about how our humanity is one that is caught up in one another's.[1]

Furthermore, Alex Boraine, who was the TRC vice chairman, has written that the TRC reflected the *ubuntu* philosophy:

> In reflecting the *ubuntu* philosophy, the Truth and Reconciliation Commission pointed to the need for more community-oriented jurisprudence that acknowledges the reality that individuals are part of a much larger social context.[2]

Many scholars have echoed Tutu's and Boraine's view that there is a close link between the TRC and *ubuntu*.[3] As highlighted in chapter one, Krog even claims that *ubuntu* was the essence and foundation of the TRC process. To support this interpretation, she provides an analysis of TRC victim testimonies during the second week of hearings, which demonstrates that at least nine direct references were made to interconnectedness that week, including the following examples:

1. ... we need to keep reminding ourselves we do belong in one family. And to help those who lost their humanity to recover their old (*Chairperson Tutu to Kwisomba family*)
2. This is not just your pain, it is shared by all of us (*Tutu to Ms Gishi*)
3. Your wound is ours too (*Commissioner Ntsebeza to Juqu family*)[4]

Surely such statements are references to interconnectedness. However, data from only one week of hearings hardly tells us much about whether or not *ubuntu* was the foundation and essence of a commission that conducted hearings for more than four years. Furthermore, none of the statements quoted by Krog in her article contain the word *ubuntu*, and whether they have anything to do with *ubuntu* at all depends on the interpretation of what *ubuntu* is. Krog interprets *ubuntu* as a worldview about interconnectedness. This is only one among several differing interpretations of *ubuntu* and—as suggested by my historical findings, presented in chapter 6—an interpretation first presented in writings in the 1990s.

THE WORD *UBUNTU* IN TRC DOCUMENTS

Krog does not explore the actual use of the word *ubuntu* in the TRC hearings; nor is she alone in that regard. Though numerous claims have been made about *ubuntu* and the TRC, no one seems to have investigated how the word was used in the TRC process, making it unclear what roles were being played in the process by explicit references to *ubuntu*. I therefore decided to explore the use of the word *ubuntu* myself by searching for it in the approximately 10,000 documents on the official TRC website. I found that among these documents, which include the transcripts of the TRC hearings, workshop transcripts, media articles, and statements, etc., fifty-four documents contain the word.[5]

The oldest of the fifty-four documents is the interim constitution of 1993, which—as already mentioned in chapters one and two—states that in addressing the strife and divisions of the apartheid past, "there is a need for understanding but not for vengeance, a need for reparation but not for retaliation, a need for *ubuntu* but not for victimization." Eighteen documents on the TRC website quote this constitutional claim for a "need for *ubuntu*" without offering any thoughts on what *ubuntu* is or why it might be needed.[6] Thus a considerable proportion of the fifty-four documents include the word *ubuntu* only because of a reference to the interim constitution.

The constitutional claim for "a need for *ubuntu*" is quoted in different kinds of texts. For instance, it appears in transcripts of amnesty hearings in situations where lawyers of perpetrators refer to the interim constitution.[7] The "need for *ubuntu*" is also quoted in the 1996 case *Azanian Peoples Organization and Others v. The President of South Africa and Others*, in which the Constitutional Court adjudicated that the TRC amnesty is constitutional—something that had been challenged by the applicants.[8] In this Court case, it is also stated that "those who negotiated the [Interim] Constitution made a deliberate choice, preferring understanding over vengeance, reparation over retaliation, *ubuntu* over victimization" (§ 19), and it is noted that this deliberate choice was historic (§ 48). The case includes no additional information on *ubuntu*.

Among the TRC staff, it was primarily Tutu who referred to *ubuntu* during hearings. In fact, I have found only one case where another commissioner—more specifically Khoza Mgojo, whom I quoted in chapter three—mentioned *ubuntu*. As will be unfolded in the following, there were also victims and perpetrators who referred to *ubuntu* in hearings, and *ubuntu* was mentioned in TRC workshops. For instance, during the workshop in Bloemfontein on July 29, 1997, Professor Sidilwane stated: "I get mad when people start speaking very glibly about *ubuntu* without really going deeply to find out what it is."[9] He added: "It [*ubuntu*] is that mysterious, if you want it, bewitchment with which we are born as sons of soil and daughters of the soil of Africa." Besides this sentence, Sidilwane offered no further information about *ubuntu*, meaning that he himself could be accused of speaking glibly about *ubuntu*. There was no further mention of *ubuntu* during that workshop.

The first time the word *ubuntu* was used in a TRC victim hearing was in the case of M. A. Tiro on April 29, 1996.[10] Here, Tutu gave an opening speech in which he proclaimed that the South African nation and indeed the world had been touched by what they had heard in the previous hearings. "We have been deeply moved by the stories of quite remarkable people, who despite their ghastly experiences harbor no hatred or bitterness," he said. He continued: "On the contrary they want to know the truth so that they should know whom they should forgive." Against this background, Tutu proclaimed: "There is a nobility of spirit in our land and we must give thanks to God for this extraordinary spirit, this wonderful *ubuntu*." Thus in this case Tutu used a reference to *ubuntu* to praise the forgiving victims. It could be argued that by articulating a close link between forgiveness and *ubuntu*, Tutu was putting pressure on victims to forgive—something he has been accused of doing.[11]

In two hearings, Tutu acknowledged that specific victims displayed *ubuntu*. This happened in a victim hearing in Worcester on June 25, 1996, where Pringle Ntando Mrubata, who had been shot by vigilantes, gave testimony.[12] Tutu said to him: "We are here to share with you the pain that you endured for the past few years, it is very painful to see you confined in a wheelchair but we are grateful that you could still smile with all your handsome face." He added: "We think that because of the pain that was inflicted on you, you could be a person who's always angry and bitter, but we are grateful that we can see that you have this spirit, the humanity, the *ubuntu* which we think is going to help us and assist us to heal the nation." Later, in a victim hearing in Welkom on October 9,

1996, Tutu also commended Litabe Thaele, who had told the TRC about the killing of his brother, for demonstrating *ubuntu*:

> here you are, a young man who is carrying a heavy load to look after the parents who themselves are traumatized and sick [after their son's death] and also to look after your brother's two children. And I want to commend you for the *ubuntu* to know that you are also responsible for the children of your brother if your brother is dead. We commend you for that. This model can be copied, especially by the young generation which has become so individualistic.[13]

In the same hearing, Tutu also suggested that specific perpetrators were lacking in *ubuntu*. This happened when he addressed Leeko Moleke, a victim of torture, and said: "In fact the great victims are those who tortured you because they lost all their humanity, humanness, *ubuntu*." He continued: "It is only the beasts or wild animals, which don't have the image of God, [who] could treat a person like that."

Later, in the faith community hearing in East London on November 17, 1997, it was once again suggested that perpetrators were lacking in *ubuntu*. This time, the suggestion was not made by Tutu, but by the representative of the African Traditional Religious Community, D. K. Koka, who stated that:

> those who raped women and killed innocent children, all these including the Gestapo murder squads of Vlakplaas, the Mamaselas, De Kocks, Coetzees and those of the killing fields of Natal [. . .] we find that all of them "hulle is sonder menswaardigheid [are without dignity]." They do not have a humanness, *ubuntu*, that is the problem.[14]

But perpetrators were not always presented as individuals devoid of *ubuntu*. In fact, in the amnesty hearing in Durban on August 12, 1999, Jabu Mkhwanazi commended one of the police officers who had been involved in the killing of her brother for showing *ubuntu* in pointing out the grave:

> Of course it was [war], but unfortunately my brother [an ANC activist] did not get the chance to defend himself. He was blindfolded, gagged, so he had no arms, so he was defenceless, he was killed like sheep going to an abattoir. [B]ut what I'm grateful about to these men, I don't know who it is, but one of them pointed out the grave. I'm very grateful to that one [because] otherwise we wouldn't know about this till today [. . .] I'm grateful to you. At least you did one good thing, that is *ubuntu*, that is to show us the grave so we could bury the [body] and we know where he is resting.[15]

Simon Mnyakeni, one of the perpetrators who testified to the TRC, also mentioned *ubuntu* in the amnesty hearing on November 23, 1999. He explained that while he was vice chairman of the ANC Youth League in Mandela squatter camp, two people were harassing the community. At first, "We were trying to restore *ubuntu* in them," [16] Mnyakeni said, and continued that the two individuals did not improve. Instead they committed a murder, whereupon they were beaten and burned to death by Mnyakeni and his comrades. This was one of the many grim cases of violent mob justice that occurred in South Africa.

One important question is of course to what extent *ubuntu* exists in a society like the South African one, with so much violence. This question was addressed in the faith community hearing in East London of November 17, 1997 cited above, where D. K. Koka suggested that the philosophy of *ubuntu* currently exists in the black community:

> among the black community, that philosophy [of *ubuntu*] is there, is operating. Among the white community, we are still to prove that they are one with us. And that this philosophy is not a peculiarity of the African people but as created beings.

This quote could be interpreted to suggest a value-laden dichotomy based on color: one the one hand, we have the black community where the good *ubuntu* philosophy is operating, and one the other hand we have the white community, lacking in *ubuntu*. Similar color-based dichotomies were essential to the apartheid era, but here it was just the white community that was presented as superior.

Some hearings also addressed the history of *ubuntu*. In the amnesty hearing in Cape Town on July 9, 1997, Peter Biehl, whose daughter Amy was killed in mob violence in the Gugulethu township, stated that "it is for the community of South Africa to forgive its own and this has its basis in traditions of *ubuntu* and other principles of human dignity." [17] His reference to "traditions of *ubuntu*" indicates that *ubuntu* has roots in the past. This was also suggested in the armed forces hearing in Cape Town on October 7, 1997, where an unnamed member of the delegation of the Pan Africanist Congress (PAC) proclaimed that during the apartheid conflict, the PAC had observed an ethic based on *ubuntu*:

> we did observe ethics [during the conflict], we did observe ethics. The only difference is that we did not extract those [ethical principles] from the international documents [about International Humanitarian Law] that you are talking about, because we had them in *ubuntu* [. . .] [In the PAC] we were exercising our leadership, therefore, in terms of *ubuntu*, which, actually, goes even beyond those pieces of paper that you are talking about. [18]

Nevertheless, commissioner Mgojo stated that *ubuntu* suffered during the conflict, and that the TRC attempted to restore it. In the victim hearing in Empangeni on November 5, 1996, he said: "It's obvious that a third force came between Africans and it took away *ubuntu* and the Truth Commission is trying by all means to give it back to the people, to bring *ubuntu* back to the people." [19] This idea that *ubuntu* is something which has been taken away and should be brought back is reflected in the narratives of return described in chapter two.

INTERVIEWS ON THE TRC AND UBUNTU

I will now move on to present what TRC commissioners and committee members told me in the course of interviews about *ubuntu* and the TRC. To my knowledge, my interviewees' viewpoints have not been presented to the public before. I will therefore quote extensively from my interviews, as the raw data may be of interest to others.

Mary Burton served as a commissioner in the Human Rights Violations Committee of the TRC. She told me that: "It [*ubuntu*] is of course a concept that Archbishop Tutu himself evokes often, both at the time and since then."[20] In continuation, she added:

> But I am not sure that the other commissioners ever really spoke about it. I will be quite interested to see if the records show something different. I can't remember us ever sitting down to have a discussion about what we understood by *ubuntu*. It was an unarticulated concept.[21]

Burton also told me that in her view, each person who worked in the TRC brought his or her own philosophy and beliefs to their work, and that although their very presence in the TRC might be interpreted as having a connectedness with *ubuntu*, *ubuntu* was not a daily reflection. In her own words:

> I think that people, each commissioner and everybody who worked in the Commission brought to their work their own philosophy, their own beliefs about what they were doing. But of course, their very presence there indicated a desire to be part of this process, which definitely seems to me has a connectedness with *ubuntu*. But for many people, it did not seem to be something that was either a daily reflection or a regular underpinning. So I would say that if it [*ubuntu*] was there at all, it was largely unarticulated.[22]

Glenda Wildschut, a commissioner who served on the Reparation and Rehabilitation Committee, echoed Burton's views when saying: "We did not sit down and say: how can we do this [in the spirit of] *ubuntu*? So there was not a conscious attempt to do that."[23] Ilan Lax, already quoted in chapter three, underscored that the TRC staff attempted to handle their mammoth job as efficiently as possible, and that in the context of time pressure there was no conscious attempt to apply *ubuntu* or other specific values:

> You know, when we did the work that we did, I certainly don't remember sitting down in a room together with others saying: How are we going to do this? What values are we going to espouse? We did not consciously sit down and do that at all. It was such a mammoth job that

that we had. We just said: How can we do this in an efficient way? What structure and mechanism can we use? At the same time we tried to bring our own humanity, our own sense of justice and our sense of what is right. We did not sit down and in a conscious way apply *ubuntu*, and I think that if people give you that impression. . . . Maybe they personally did, I certainly didn't.[24]

Hugh Lewin, a committee member of the Human Rights Violations Committee, agreed with Burton, Wildschut and Lax. He told me: "In my time at the Commission, the concept of *ubuntu* was not formally integrated into the organizational culture."[25] He elaborated: "By this, I mean that it [*ubuntu*] was obviously embodied by the Archbishop and some other people, particularly those who came from faith-based backgrounds, but as a concept I would say that it was more implicit, rather than explicitly identified as a definite policy."[26] In this connection, Fazel Randera, a commissioner in the Human Rights Violations Committee, also explained that *ubuntu* did not resonate with all the commissioners, and that he personally had his own view of the world:

> It may appear as if *ubuntu* became the philosophy of the TRC, but I don't think that was one that generally resonated with everybody. Personally, I had my own view of the world. When people started talking about *ubuntu*, I was trying to understand because it wasn't—let me be very honest—it wasn't part of my thinking in the 1980s or 1990s. And suddenly this concept comes about! It was not something that I would say I personally integrated into my life and said: "Ahh, this is what I would like to do."[27]

Based on my interviews, there is no reason to claim that *ubuntu* was the essence and foundation of the TRC process. On the contrary, the TRC commissioners and committee members emphasized that they did not discuss *ubuntu*, that *ubuntu* was not a definite policy of the TRC, and that the TRC staff brought their own individual beliefs to their work. However, some suggested that although *ubuntu* was not a policy of the TRC, it may have had some kind of tacit presence in the TRC process. For example, Lewin saw a link between *ubuntu* and the way Tutu led the hearings:

> Tutu chaired the Human Rights Violations Committee and he dealt with potential conflict in a very creative way. He would let the discussion flow, but when confrontation became too intense, he would say: "Oh, time for meditation." And everyone was asked to close their eyes and keep silent for a minute, which somehow took the sting out of their emotions. He did this quite often when things became really heated. Only he could have done that! He is a "politician plus": someone who understands power dynamics, but who also embodies *ubuntu* in the purest form. He had—and still has—an inner grace and strength which I think is remarkable. It is based on a very strong indignation against injustice and, at the same time, a very strong belief in humanity.[28]

Pumla Gobodo-Madikizela, who served on the Human Rights Violations Committee, also suggested that *ubuntu* was reflected in the setting of the TRC, in the sense that the process was designed in such a way that it allowed the perpetrators to become human, to bring out their humanity:

> It [the setting of the Commission] is created in such a way that I am invited to tell the truth commission what happened. When inviting someone, even perpetrators, you invite them to reflect about the aspects of their humanness, so that when they enter the stage, they enter the stage with the expectation that they will be treated as human beings. Now, if you treat someone else as a human being, you are forcing them to reflect in a moral sense, to reflect on the terrible things they did in the context of the wrongness of their deeds. Why? Because the starting point is that you treat them as human beings. So there, *ubuntu* is to allow this person to become a human being. You are making it possible for them to bring out their humanity.[29]

Burton also explained that, in her view, *ubuntu* shone through in the telling and hearing of stories. In order to explain what she meant she elaborated on the notion of reconciliation, and told me a story about a young white man who joined the South African army and a young black man who joined the guerrilla forces:

> I have not [previously] been asked before about the meaning of *ubuntu*, but I have been asked often about the meaning of "reconciliation." What do I think that reconciliation is? And my answer has always been that if you could take a young white man who joined the South African army and was trained to fight against the external threat—as he perceived it, as his society and his world perceived it. . . . And at the same time you could expose him to a young man who had decided to go to exile joining the guerrilla forces and be trained to fight. . . . And you could get them to talk to each other, and each to understand the other's experience—not necessary condone it or agree with it, but to understand it. . . . I think that would be the beginning of reconciliation. And I think that has a sense of *ubuntu* about it—of reaching out to the other person. So in that sense I think that *ubuntu* was lived out in the telling of stories and the hearing of stories.[30]

Additionally, there were commissioners who emphasized that in their view, *ubuntu* was reflected in the behavior of victims. In this connection, we should recall that during the hearings, Tutu occasionally praised the *ubuntu* of forgiving victims. Mgojo argued that there is a close link between *ubuntu* and forgiveness, but he emphasized that the commissioners had to be careful not to put pressure on the victims by suggesting that they had to forgive:

> Of course you must articulate *ubuntu*! I mean, when those families say: "Thank you, you are forgiven." There were some who said that after they had come angry. They said: "Okay, we are forgiving this person." To me, they were driven by *ubuntu*, because it [*ubuntu*] has to come out,

you can't internalize it! It is something which you cannot internalize — you must voice it out. But you had to be careful. The victims had to come to that conclusion themselves, without you suggesting it. That would be dangerous! You had to work through them, so that it comes from them. "Mr Commissioner, I think I am healed, this has helped me, and I am willing to forgive this person."[31]

Dumisa Ntsebeza, the commissioner who led the TRC Investigative Unit, told me about a victim called Beth Savage, whose conduct he saw as an expression of *ubuntu*. What is particularly thought-provoking about this story is that Beth asks to meet her perpetrators in order to ask them for forgiveness:

> There was a woman who came to us as a victim — a white woman. Beth Savage is her name. Beth Savage is from East London. She was sitting at a restaurant, like any other normal person in a normal society would be doing, when there was an attack at the restaurant. She was terribly injured; in fact she was fortunate to have kept her life. She underwent multiple operations. There she was, now coming to us to talk about how it was to have been a victim. Now, when she ended her testimony to us, she said. . . . You know, because we used to ask the question: "What would you like the TRC to do?" Do you know what she said? She said: "I would like to meet the people who did this." That was a normal request. So we said: "Oh yeah, we will make arrangements. Anything in particular, you want them to say?" We had thought that she would like to meet them because she would like to know from them why they did this thing to her. She was innocent, you know! But she goes further — she says: "Yeah, that is one of the reasons. I would certainly like to know what caused them to do this, but so that I also can ask them to forgive me!"
>
> Then we thought that we had not heard right! "You want to ask them. . . ?" She said, "Yes," and we said: "But we cannot understand!" And she said: "You know what: as a white woman who grew up in South Africa, who had the privileges that we had which black people didn't, who was able to vote when they could not, and through my vote I could return the Nationalist Party's government in election after election — maybe there is something that I did not do right as a white person in South Africa. And that is why I want to ask these people to forgive me because there must be something I presented as a white person here in South Africa . . . [which caused] people to be so desperate as to go and shoot people."
>
> That was very profound! Here is a person who was a victim, who goes beyond the anger of having been a victim, and she says: "I want to be reconciled with my perpetrators because I owe them something." That is something that you cannot explain, and it can only be because of that central element of *ubuntu*! Not just as an issue of justice, but as an issue of humanness! We arranged for her to meet with them, and it turned out that the guy who had been the commander of the unit that had attacked the restaurant came to testify because he wanted to apply

for amnesty. And this guy said: "Look, I am sorry that it happened, but we were at war and . . ." After that she [Beth Savage] had a press interview—days after that—and she said: "Since I met my perpetrator something happened! Up to that time when I met him and where I had this exchange with him, I had nightmares about that night when it happened every night! But since I had that discussion, it has not been like that.[32]

Bongani Finca, who served as a commissioner in the Human Rights Violations Committee, agreed with Ntsebeza that *ubuntu* informed the conduct of some victims, and he added that in his experience it was first and foremost the victims who had suffered the most who showed *ubuntu*. Through his experiences as a TRC commissioner, he had got a sense that people who had gone through intense suffering themselves were more sensitive to the pain of others:

> I think that the people who challenged me a great deal in my work as a commissioner were mainly the people who had suffered more than others and continued to suffer even after 1994. I would expect those people to be very bitter, but they had been taught through their experience of suffering to value *ubuntu*. I find that there is a sense in which those who have suffered the most seem to have been taught by their experience of suffering generally to be more accommodating. People who have suffered a little seem to me to be capable of calling for more revenge than people who have suffered more than others. That to me sort of made me feel that there is something about going through intense suffering which makes you even more sensitive to the pain of others because of the intensity of the pain that you have gone through yourself. . . . It was those who had suffered most deeply who were able to do amazing, unbelievable things of stretching out their hands and holding them out to those to whom they had every right to say: "I don't want to have anything to do with you after what you did to me!" They were able to stretch out their hands and offer forgiveness. It was an amazing experience that I went through.[33]

In Finca's view, the TRC would have failed had it not been for the *ubuntu* shown by victims. However, he also explained that many of the perpetrators who testified to the TRC failed to show *ubuntu*, and that this made the victims bitter. They stretched out their hands in forgiveness, but were not met in an appropriate way by the perpetrators:

> I do not see *ubuntu* as the product of the Truth Commission, which means that people started without *ubuntu* and because of the Truth Commission became. . . . I say that the Truth Commission was made possible by people coming holding this *ubuntu* already in their hearts. It was made possible by that. Without that *ubuntu* in them, the Truth Commission would have failed. Because how do we start even to engage with the kinds of things that we engage with . . . ? How did people come and open up in the manner in which they opened up, unless they

already have the understanding that for the restoration of relationships in this country, I need to be able to rise above my anger in order to embrace other people?

My sense is that the attitude especially of those who had the responsibility to ask for forgiveness and failed to ask for forgiveness actually may have challenged even those who had *ubuntu* to become bitter even in spite of that. Because here they are, so keen to say to Christian: "I embrace you as my brother although you did this to me." And here is Christian saying. . . . You had to stretch out toward him [the perpetrator], but he is not able to take that hand. You who are so driven by the spirit of *ubuntu* to embrace, to forgive, find that the person who you want to forgive is actually not ready to say: "Can you forgive?"[34]

In continuation, Finca explained that moments of celebration of *ubuntu* were rare, and that some perpetrators simply came to the TRC because they wanted their crimes expunged from their records, not because they were led by *ubuntu*:

There were moments of celebration of *ubuntu*, moments of victims and perpetrators embracing each other, and I know that out of that, the spirit of *ubuntu* was promoted. But to me those moments were very few. In most cases. . . I mean: if you read the legislation, the Promotion of National Unity and Reconciliation Act, it did not require a person who is applying for amnesty to say: "I am sorry."

Gade: Why was that? Why did it not require that?

Finca: We were told that the people who drafted the legislation felt that you cannot legislate a thing like remorse. Remorse is something that you feel inside. So if you are drafting legislation and say: "One of the requirements is that a person must show remorse. . . ." They felt that remorse is something that belongs to the inside of the person.

So these people [the perpetrators] would come in. They were required to tell what they did, they are required to tell it truthfully, they are required to show that they were motivated by a political aim. There was no requirement of them to say: "I am actually very sorry for what I did." And some of them really did not, in my view, come to those hearings led by *ubuntu*. They came there because they wanted to have the crimes they had done expunged from their records. They came there because some of them were in jail, and they wanted to be released earlier. If they had come there with the spirit of seeking healing of the community, if they had come there with the spirit of *ubuntu*, there would have been a potential for such a wave of new life and new attitudes to spread to our society. The atmosphere was ready, and the victims were ready, but my sense is that the perpetrators missed the opportunity to show *ubuntu*! Whether they embraced the concept of *ubuntu*, I don't know, but they missed the opportunity.[35]

LOOKING BACK AT THE TRC

In the actual TRC hearings, no one presented the view that *ubuntu* was the essence and foundation of the TRC process. The closest we got to such a view is the quoted statement from commissioner Mgojo, who said that the TRC had tried to bring *ubuntu* back to the people. Furthermore, based on the data that I have presented in this chapter, we have no good reason to suggest that *ubuntu* talk was used to "sell" the TRC in the hearings. It could with some reason be argued that *ubuntu* talk was used to encourage or even put pressure on victims to forgive, but even this may be an over-interpretation, as there were only a few references to *ubuntu* in relation to forgiveness during the TRC process.

Despite the above-mentioned findings, it has—as I have emphasized—frequently been claimed that there was a very close connection between the TRC and *ubuntu*. In this connection, it is important to be aware that most of the claims about such a close connection have been made since the TRC process, meaning that they represent *retrospective* interpretations by people looking back at the TRC. Those who retrospectively connect *ubuntu* and the TRC may have different agendas, and it is difficult—sometimes maybe even impossible—to know what their specific agendas are in concrete cases. When I read Antjie Krog's 2008 article, in which she states that *ubuntu* was the essence and foundation of the TRC process, my sense is that she simply connects the TRC and *ubuntu* because she truly believes that *ubuntu* is of key importance if we want to understand the TRC process. As I read the article, it is not an attempt to legitimize this process. Tutu's statement, cited in the beginning of this chapter, that "we were actually using the principles of *ubuntu*" could, on the other hand, very well be an attempt to legitimize the TRC, as the statement was made in a context where the TRC amnesty was accused of sacrificing justice.

Ubuntu can be used as a tool for legitimization, and thus we should be critical when someone states that specific practices, political programs, etc. are in agreement with *ubuntu*. Furthermore, *ubuntu* has become a very fluffy concept defined in various ways, and thus it is extremely easy to claim that something is an expression of *ubuntu*. In this connection, Lax told me that: "You can find *ubuntu* in many things that we did, but we didn't realize that or consciously make it *ubuntu*."[36] Furthermore, he explained: "When you sit and reflect on that [TRC experience] backwards, you can see that there are elements where you can say: Yes, this reflects *ubuntu* in many respects." However, Burton emphasized that though it is possible and quite easy to read *ubuntu* into the process, it is important to recognize that not everything in the TRC was conducted in a spirit of *ubuntu*:

Because, quite honestly, many people in the Truth Commission were much more cynical than that, much more skeptical than that. Yes, they were not going to contradict concepts of *ubuntu* and so on—but they were by no means convinced that restorative justice was good enough. If you think about the Investigative Unit and the desire to—if not punish perpetrators, then at least to bring them into the public eye, humiliate them. . . . There was a kind of desire to see them "put down," you might say—which would be in conflict, I think, with a real, true spirit of *ubuntu*. So I would be very anxious not to make a claim that everything was conducted in the spirit of *ubuntu*. But nevertheless, some of those things. . . . Being in Africa, many of us, many of them, the people in the Commission—staff as well as commissioners—had that [*ubuntu*] in their collective history. So it probably does have an influence, even if it wasn't really recognized at the time.[37]

But is Burton even correct in suggesting that people in South Africa have *ubuntu* as part of their collective history, and what exactly does it mean that something is part of a collective history? Certainly, *ubuntu* ideas are not part of a collective history in the sense of constituting a static set of ideas inherited from previous generations. In fact, the widespread ethnophilosophical approach to ideas as a static group property is highly problematic, as I argue in the next chapter, where I delve deeper into the issue of African philosophy.

NOTES

1. Desmond Tutu in Institute for Justice and Reconciliation, "Truth, Justice, Memory: South Africa's Truth and Reconciliation Process," (documentary by the Institute for Justice and Reconciliation, Cape Town, 2008), episode 1.

2. Alex Boraine, *A Country Unmasked: Inside South Africa's Truth and Reconciliation Commission* (Oxford: Oxford University Press, 2000), 425.

3. For example, see Nomonde Masina, "Xhosa Practices of *Ubuntu* for South Africa," in *Traditional Cures for Modern Conflicts: African Conflict "Medicine,"* ed. William Zartman (London: Lynne Rienner, 2000); Lyn S. Graybill, *Truth and Reconciliation in South Africa: Miracle or Model?* (Boulder and London: Lynne Rienner Publishers, 2002); Timothy Murithi, "Practical Peacemaking Wisdom from Africa: Reflections on *Ubuntu*," *The Journal of Pan African Studies* 1, no. 4 (2006).

4. Antjie Krog, "'This Thing Called Reconciliation . . . ' Forgiveness as Part of an Interconnectedness-Towards-Wholeness," South African Journal of Philosophy 27, no. 4 (2008): 358.

5. In chronological order, these texts are:

Constitution of the Republic of South Africa, Act No. 200 of 1993, http://www.justice.gov.za/trc/legal/sacon93.htm;
Promotion of National Unity and Reconciliation Bill, No. 30 (1995), http://www.justice.gov.za/trc/legal/b30_95.htm;
Explanatory Memorandum to the Parliamentary Bill (1995), http://www.justice.gov.za/trc/legal/bill.htm;
Promotion of National Unity and Reconciliation, Act 34 of 1995 (1995), http://www.justice.gov.za/legislation/acts/1995-034.pdf;

Justice in Transition, booklet explaining the role of the TRC (1995), http://www.justice.gov.za/trc/legal/justice.htm;

TRC: Victim Hearing, Day 1 in Johannesburg, Before the Human Rights Violation Committee, No. GO/00 (Apr. 29, 1996) (Hearing of M. A. Tiro), http://www.justice.gov.za/trc/hrvtrans%5Cmethodis/tiro.htm;

TRC: Amnesty Hearing, Day 1 in Phokeng, Before the Amnesty Committee, No. 0081/96 and No. 0080/96 (May 20, 1996) (B. Diali and C. Mokgatle), http://www.justice.gov.za/trc/amntrans/phokeng/phokeng.htm;

TRC: Victim Hearing, Day 2 in Worcester, Cape Town, Before the Human Rights Violation Committee, No. CT/00130 (June 25, 1996) (Hearing of P. Mrubata), http://www.justice.gov.za/trc/hrvtrans%5Cworcest/ct00130.htm;

Azanian Peoples Organization and Others v. The President of South Africa and Others, No. CCT 17/96 (Constitutional Court of South Africa, Decided July 25, 1996), http://www.justice.gov.za/trc/legal/azapo.htm;

Mr. F. W. De Klerk, leader of the National Party, Submission to the TRC (Aug., 1996), http://www.justice.gov.za/trc/hrvtrans/submit/np_truth.htm;

The African Christian Democratic Party, ACDP, Submission to the TRC, Day 1 in Cape Town, Political Party Hearings, (Aug. 19, 1996), http://www.justice.gov.za/trc/special%5Cparty1/acdp.htm;

Reparation and Rehabilitation Committee, "Policy Framework for Urgent Interim Reparation Measures," (Policy Documents, Sep. 14, 1996), http://www.justice.gov.za/trc/reparations/policy.htm;

TRC: Victim Hearings, Day 2 in Welkom, Durban, Before the Human Rights Violation Committee, No. FS/TDM/006, No. FS/MBL/024 and No. FS/TDM/011, (Oct. 9, 1996) (Hearings of L. Moleke, L. Thaele and P. Morake), http://www.justice.gov.za/trc/hrvtrans%5Cwelkom/welkom2.htm;

TRC: Victim Hearing, Day 2 in Empangeni, Durban, Before the Human Rights Violation Committee, (Nov. 5, 1996) (Hearing of E. Simelane), 108–21, http://www.justice.gov.za/trc/hrvtrans%5Cempang/empang2.htm;

"Make Perpetrators Pay for Misdeeds: Ngewu," *South Africa Press Association, SAPA*, Cape Town, Mar. 19, 1997, http://www.justice.gov.za/trc/media/1997/9703/s970319c.htm;

TRC: Follow up Workshop Transcript, Reiger Park in Boksburg (Apr. 19, 1997), http://www.justice.gov.za/trc/reparations/reiger.htm;

"High Price for Freedom Paid says Tutu at Memorial Opening," *SAPA*, Bisho, Apr. 21, 1997, http://www.justice.gov.za/trc/media/1997/9704/s970421e.htm;

"TRC to Ring Apartheid," *SAPA*, Cape Town, Apr. 21, 1997, http://www.justice.gov.za/trc/media%5C1997%5C9704/s970421a.htm;

TRC: Children's Hearings, Day 3 in Cape Town, Letter from Rudie-Lee Reagan (May 22, 1997), http://www.justice.gov.za/trc/special%5Cchildren/reagan.htm;

"TRC's Focus on the Role of Children and Youth," *TRC Press Release*, June 3, 1997, http://www.justice.gov.za/trc/media/pr/1997/p970603a.htm;

TRC: Victim Hearing, Day 1 in Leandra, Johannesburg, Before the Human Rights Violation Committee, No. JB0283 (June 3, 1997) (Hearing of S. P. Molokoane), http://www.justice.gov.za/trc/hrvtrans%5Cleandra/molokoan.htm;

TRC: Follow up Workshop Transcript, Sebokeng College (June 21, 1997), http://www.justice.gov.za/trc/reparations/sebokeng.htm;

TRC: Amnesty Hearing, Day 3 in Cape Town, Before the Amnesty Committee, Case Killing of Amy Biehl, Part 2 (July 9, 1997) (Hearing of S. Ntamo), http://www.justice.gov.za/trc/amntrans%5Ccapetown/capetown_biehl02.htm;

TRC: Conscription Hearings, Cape Town, Special Submission on Conscription, (July 23, 1997), Part 2, http://www.justice.gov.za/trc/special%5Cconscrip/conscr02.htm;

TRC: Workshop Transcript, Bloenfontein (July 29, 1997), http://www.justice.gov.za/trc/reparations/bloem.htm;

TRC: Armed Forces Hearings, Day 1 in Cape Town, PAC / APLA (Oct. 7, 1997), http://www.justice.gov.za/trc/special%5Cforces/apla.htm;

TRC: Faith Communities Hearing, Day 1–3 in East London (Nov. 17–19, 1997), http://www.justice.gov.za/trc/special%5Cfaith/faith_a.htm and http://www.justice.gov.za/Trc/special/faith/faith_b.htm;

TRC: Victim Hearing, Day 1 first session in Johannesburg, Mandela United Football Club Hearings (Nov. 24, 1997) (Hearing of N. Z. W. Madikizela-Mandela), http://www.justice.gov.za/trc/special%5Cmandela/mufc1.htm;

TRC: Victim Hearing, Day 5 first session in Johannesburg, Mandela United Football Club Hearings (Nov. 28, 1997), http://www.justice.gov.za/trc/special%5Cmandela/mufc5a.htm;

General G. L. Meiring, Chief of SANDF, South African National Defense Force, Address to the TRC (1997), http://www.justice.gov.za/trc/hrvtrans/submit/sandf.htm;

TRC: Reparation and Rehabilitation Workshop Transcript, Day 3 in Johannesburg (Feb. 20, 1998), http://www.justice.gov.za/trc/reparations/joburg3.htm;

TRC: Amnesty Hearing, Day 4 at Richards Bay in Durban, Before the Amnesty Committee, Case: Attack on Flagstaff Police Station, Part 4–5 (Apr. 14, 1998) (Hearing of B. Q. Mkhize), http://www.justice.gov.za/trc/amntrans%5Cdurban/dbn2.htm;

TRC: Amnesty Hearing, Day 1 in East London, Before the Amnesty Committee, Case: Murder of Donnie and Mike Meyers (May 25, 1998) (Hearing of Z. Tuta and N. Kulman), http://www.justice.gov.za/trc/amntrans%5Cel/elnma27.htm;

TRC: Amnesty Hearing, Day 4 in Ermelo, Before the Amnesty Committee (July 23, 1998) (Hearing of M. Gushu), http://www.justice.gov.za/trc//amntrans/amntrans-pdfs/trc-amntrans-am1998-Ermelo-01.pdf;

TRC: Amnesty Decision, No. AC/98/0030 (July 28, 1998), http://www.justice.gov.za/trc/decisions%5C1998/980728_ntamo%20penietc.htm;

"Amnesty for Killers of Amy Biehl," *TRC Press Release*, July 28, 1998, http://www.justice.gov.za/trc/media/pr/1998/p980728a.htm;

TRC Final Report, "Summary and Guide to Contents," (Oct., 1998), http://www.justice.gov.za/trc/report/execsum.htm;

TRC Final Report, Vol. 1, (Oct., 1998), http://www.justice.gov.za/trc/report/finalreport/Volume%201.pdf;

TRC Final Report, Vol. 4, (Oct., 1998), http://www.justice.gov.za/trc/report/finalreport/Volume%204.pdf;

TRC Final Report, Vol. 5, (Oct., 1998), http://www.justice.gov.za/trc/report/finalreport/Volume5.pdf;

TRC: Amnesty Hearing, Day 6 in Pretoria, Before the Amnesty Committee, Case: London Bomb, (Mar. 1, 1999), http://www.justice.gov.za/trc/amntrans%5C1999/9902220304_pre_990301pt.htm;

TRC: Amnesty Hearing, Day 3 in East London, Before the Amnesty Committee, Case: Operation Katzen (Apr. 8, 1999), http://www.justice.gov.za/trc/amntrans%5C1999/99040608_el_990408el.htm;

TRC: Amnesty Hearing, Day 6 in Johannesburg, Before the Amnesty Committee, No. AM2880/96 (Apr. 20, 1999) (Hearing of M. Bellingan), http://www.justice.gov.za/trc/amntrans%5C1999/99041220_jhb_990420jb.htm;

TRC: Amnesty Hearing, Day 3 in Durban, Before the Amnesty Committee, No. AM4077/96, (Aug. 12, 1999) (Hearing of J. A. Vorster), http://www.justice.gov.za/trc/amntrans%5C1999/9908100903_dbn_990812db.htm;

TRC: Amnesty Hearing, Day 1 in Durban, Before the Amnesty Committee, No. AM5637/97 (Oct. 18, 1999) (Hearing of J. M. Van Zyl), http://www.justice.gov.za/trc/amntrans%5C1999/99101819_dbn_991018.htm;

TRC: Amnesty Hearing, Day 4 in Cape Town, Before the Amnesty Committee, No. AM7997/97 (Oct. 21, 1999) (Hearing of I. P. Siyali), http://www.justice.gov.za/trc/amntrans/1999/99101828_ct_991021.htm;

TRC: *Amnesty Hearing, Day 1 in Johannesburg, Before the Amnesty Committee*, No. AM5878/97 (Nov. 23, 1999) (Hearing of S. M. Hlophe), http://www.justice.gov.za/trc/amntrans%5C1999/99112325_jhb_991123jb.htm;

TRC: *Amnesty Decision*, No. AC/99/00031, App.No. AM2773/96, (1999) (App.: J. H. Cronje), http://www.justice.gov.za/trc/decisions%5C1999/99_cronje.html;

TRC: *Amnesty Hearing, Day 2 in Pretoria, Before the Amnesty Committee*, Case: Simelane Matter, (May 30, 2000), http://www.justice.gov.za/trc/amntrans/2000/200530pt.htm;

TRC: *Amnesty Hearing, Day 23 in Cape Town, Before the Amnesty Committee*, Case: CCB Hearing (Nov. 18, 2000), http://www.justice.gov.za/trc/amntrans%5C2000/2001118.htm;

TRC Final Report, Vol. 6, Sec. 1, (Mar., 2003), http://www.justice.gov.za/trc/report/finalreport/vol6_s1.pdf; TRC Report, Vol. 6, Sec. 2, (Mar., 2003), http://www.justice.gov.za/trc/report/finalreport/vol6_s2.pdf; TRC Report, Vol. 6, Sec. 3, (Mar., 2003), http://www.justice.gov.za/trc/report/finalreport/vol6_s3.pdf.

6. *Promotion Bill*, No. 30 (1995); *Explanatory Memorandum* (1995); *Promotion*, Act 34 of 1995 (1995); *Justice in Transition*, (1995); *Amnesty Hearing, Phokeng*, No. 0081/96 and No. 0080/96 (May 20, 1996); De Klerk, *Submission* (Aug., 1996); Reparation and Rehabilitation Comm., *Policy Framework*, (Sep. 14, 1996); *Follow up Workshop*, Boksburg, (Apr. 19, 1997); *Victim Hearing, Johannesburg*, (Nov. 24, 1997); *Victim Hearing, Johannesburg*, (Nov. 28, 1997); Meiring, *Address* (1997); *Amnesty Hearing, Pretoria*, Case: London Bomb, (Mar. 1, 1999); *Amnesty Hearing, East London*, Case: Operation Katzen (Apr. 8, 1999); *Amnesty Hearing, Johannesburg*, No. AM2880/96 (Apr. 20, 1999); *Amnesty Decision*, No. AC/99/00031, (1999); *Amnesty Hearing, Pretoria*, Case: Simelane Matter, (May 30, 2000); *Amnesty Hearing, Cape Town*, Case: CCB (Nov. 18, 2000); *TRC Final Report*, Vol. 6, Sec. 1, (Mar., 2003).

7. B. Currin in *Amnesty Hearing, Phokeng*, No. 0081/96 and No. 0080/96 (May 20, 1996); N. Arendse in *Amnesty Hearing, Cape Town*, Amy Biehl part 2 (July 9, 1997); B. Knoetze in *Amnesty Hearing, East London*, Case: Operation Katzen (Apr. 8, 1999); Mr Wessel in *Amnesty Hearing, Cape Town*, Case: CCB (Nov. 18, 2000).

8. See *Azanian Peoples Organization*, No. CCT 17/96.

9. See TRC: Workshop Transcript, Bloenfontein (July 29, 1997), http://www.justice.gov.za/trc/reparations/bloem.htm.

10. See *Victim Hearing, Johannesburg*, Hearing of M. A. Tiro (Apr. 29, 1996).

11. See Thomas Brudholm, *Resentment's Virtue: Jean Améry and the Refusal to Forgive* (Philadelphia: Temple University Press, 2008). Concerning the pressure on victims to forgive, Tutu has been quoted for making the following remark in an interview: "In our understanding, when someone doesn't forgive, we say that person does not have *ubuntu*. That is to say he is not really human." Richard Bell, *Rethinking Justice: Restoring Our Humanity* (Lanham, MD: Lexington Books, 2007), 54.

12. See TRC: *Victim Hearing, Day 2 in Worcester, Cape Town, Before the Human Rights Violation Committee*, No. CT/00130 (June 25, 1996) (Hearing of P. Mrubata), http://www.justice.gov.za/trc/hrvtrans%5Cworcest/ct00130.htm.

13. See TRC: *Victim Hearings, Day 2 in Welkom, Durban, Before the Human Rights Violation Committee*, No. FS/TDM/006, No. FS/MBL/024 and No. FS/TDM/011, (Oct. 9, 1996) (Hearings of L. Moleke, L. Thaele and P. Morake), http://www.justice.gov.za/trc/hrvtrans%5Cwelkom/welkom2.htm.

14. See TRC: *Faith Communities Hearing, Day 1–3 in East London* (Nov. 17–19, 1997), http://www.justice.gov.za/trc/special%5Cfaith/faith_a.htm and http://www.justice.gov.za/Trc/special/faith/faith_b.htm.

15. See TRC: *Amnesty Hearing, Day 3 in Durban, Before the Amnesty Committee*, No. AM4077/96, (Aug. 12, 1999) (Hearing of J. A. Vorster), http://www.justice.gov.za/trc/amntrans%5C1999/9908100903_dbn_990812db.htm.

16. See *TRC: Amnesty Hearing, Day 1 in Johannesburg, Before the Amnesty Committee*, No. AM5878/97 (Nov. 23, 1999) (Hearing of S. M. Hlophe), http://www.justice.gov.za/trc/amntrans%5C1999/99112325_jhb_991123jb.htm.

17. See *TRC: Amnesty Hearing, Day 3 in Cape Town, Before the Amnesty Committee*, Case Killing of Amy Biehl, Part 2 (July 9, 1997) (Hearing of S. Ntamo), http://www.justice.gov.za/trc/amntrans%5Ccapetown/capetown_biehl02.htm.

18. See *TRC: Armed Forces Hearings, Day 1 in Cape Town*, PAC / APLA (Oct. 7, 1997), http://www.justice.gov.za/trc/special%5Cforces/apla.htm.

19. See *TRC: Victim Hearing, Day 2 in Empangeni, Durban, Before the Human Rights Violation Committee*, (Nov. 5, 1996) (Hearing of E. Simelane), 108–121, http://www.justice.gov.za/trc/hrvtrans%5Cempang/empang2.htm.

20. Mary Burton, interviewed by author, Sep. 29, 2008, Cape Town.
21. Ibid.
22. Ibid.
23. Wildschut, interview.
24. Lax, interview.
25. Hugh Lewin, interviewed by author, Nov. 20, 2008, Johannesburg.
26. Ibid.
27. Fazel Randera, interviewed by author, Nov. 23, 2008, Johannesburg.
28. Lewin, interview.
29. Pumla Gobodo-Madikizela, interviewed by author, Aug. 27, 2008, Cape Town.
30. Burton, interview.
31. Mgojo, interview.
32. Dumisa Ntsebeza, interviewed by author, Nov. 24, 2008, Johannesburg.
33. Bongani Finca, interviewed by author, Nov. 26, 2008, Durban.
34. Ibid.
35. Ibid.
36. Lax, interview.
37. Burton, interview.

FIVE
Ethnophilosophy
The Myth of Shared Static Ideas

Compared to the written history of Western philosophy, which dates back to the pre-Socratic thinkers of classical antiquity, the written history of African philosophy is very young. It is normally held to begin with Tempels's ethnophilosophical book *Bantu Philosophy* (*La Philosophie Bantoue* in French), dating from 1945. Prior to Tempels' book, African scholars had not yet addressed the topic of African philosophy, and European scholars did not seem to take seriously the possibility that Africans could be capable of the rational activity of philosophizing. Throughout the colonial period it was common to perceive Africans as rationally inferior beings in need of "help" from Europeans in the form of education and governance. This attitude was also present within Western philosophy, and can be identified in the writings of some of the most famous Western thinkers such as Hume, Kant, and Hegel.[1] For example, in "Of National Characters" in the 1758 edition of *Essays and Treatises on Several Subjects*, Hume writes:

> I am apt to suspect the negroes, and in general all the other species of men (for there are four or five different kinds) to be naturally inferior to the whites. There never was a civilized nation of any other complexion than white, nor even any individual eminent either in action or speculation. No ingenious manufactures amongst them, no arts, no science. On the other hand, the most rude and barbarous of the whites, such as the ancient Germans, the present Tartars, have still something eminent about them, in their valor, form of government, or some other particular.[2]

PLACIDE TEMPELS' BANTU PHILOSOPHY

Tempels was a Belgian Franciscan missionary working in the Belgian Congo from 1933 to 1962. His *Bantu Philosophy* should be read in the context of the long history of racism against blacks. The book is a child of this history in the sense that Tempels continues the tradition of describing the relationship between Africans and Europeans as fundamentally unequal; in his view, the former are primitives who must be civilized, taught, and educated by the latter. However, the book can also to some extent be read as a rebellion against the aforementioned history, because it challenges the common view at the time that Africans lacked the ability of logical thinking. Tempels writes: "To declare on a priori grounds that primitive peoples have no ideas on the nature of beings, that they have no ontology and that they are completely lacking in logic, is simply to turn one's back to reality."[3]

At the beginning of his book, Tempels characterizes the behavior of the Bantu as "a universal system of human behavior."[4] He claims that such a system of permanent and universal behavior can only exist if it is based upon a complete philosophy of the universe, "of man and of the things which surrounds him, of existence, life, death, and the life beyond."[5] Therefore, Tempels is convinced that the Bantu have a philosophy, even though he underscores its primitiveness and simplicity.[6] Primitive as it might be, however, Europeans ought to understand the Bantu philosophy, according to Tempels, since only through this philosophy is it possible to infiltrate the native thought.[7] Perhaps most importantly: "Only if we set out from the true, the good and stable in native custom [i.e., their philosophy] shall we be able to lead our Africans to the direction of a true Bantu civilization."[8]

Throughout his book, Tempels underscores the importance of the Bantu philosophy for the life of the Bantu people. He writes that the philosophy is evident and dominant in all their thought, behavior, and knowledge.[9] Thus according to Tempels, "They have no other conception of the world,"[10] and the philosophy "directs all their activities and inactivities."[11] Nevertheless, Tempels also explains that it certainly cannot be expected, especially not from the younger generation, that Africans themselves are capable of presenting a systematic description of their own philosophy.[12] Thus it is the Europeans who should describe the Bantu philosophy:

> It is we who will be able to tell them, in precise terms, what their inmost concept of being is. They will recognize themselves in our words and will acquiesce, saying, "You understand us: you know us completely: you 'know' us in the way we 'know.'"[13]

Then Tempels begins to unfold the Bantu philosophy. He explains that the fundamental difference between Western and Bantu thought is that in the former, the concept of "being" is distinguished from "force."[14] He writes that "There is no idea among the Bantu of 'being' divorced from the idea of 'force,'"[15] and he suggests that, for the Bantu, "Force is the nature of being, force is being, being is force."[16] In Tempels' interpretation, this implies that all things, living and inanimate alike, possess a vital force: a force given by God.[17]

Tempels continues that in the Bantu philosophy, all forces are perceived as interconnected: "The world of forces is held like a spider's web of which no single thread can be caused to vibrate without shaking the whole network."[18] Thus man is not suspended in thin air: "He lives on his land, where he finds himself to be the sovereign vital force, ruling the land and all that lives on it: man, animal, or plant."[19] The spider's web of forces is hierarchically ordered, with God as the greatest force, followed by human persons, animals, and the inanimate.

Tempels is convinced that the Bantu philosophy is "the common property of the whole Bantu society."[20] In fact, he writes that "[t]his universal wisdom is accepted by everyone, it is not subjected to criticism, it has currency, in regard to its general principles, as imperishable Truth."[21] Logically speaking, this implies—as Tempels also states—that previous generations followed this philosophy as well.[22] However, Tempels recognizes that Bantu societies are not completely static; for example, the Bantu had changed their religious practices under the influence of Christianity. Still, he insists that different practices are linked to the same Bantu philosophy, something which remains a stable and unchanging foundation of the Bantu society.[23]

CRITIQUE OF PLACIDE TEMPELS

There are many difficulties with Tempels' book, some of which are related to racial prejudices and incorrect assumptions that were current when the book was written. Of course Africans are not primitives who must be civilized, taught, and educated by Europeans. They are not "our Africans," as Tempels suggests, nor are Africans, any more than Europeans, in need of being secured a purer and more dynamic life. Furthermore, every individual knows best what his or her own thoughts are, and is in no need of being educated by Europeans in that regard. It is absurd to believe that Europeans had privileged knowledge of how Africans think, and equally absurd to believe that African philosophy could only be given a systematic exposition by Europeans.

Another problem with Tempels is that he is obsessed with systems. He claims that the behavior of the Bantu constitutes a universal system of human behavior, and that their philosophy is a logical system of thought. It almost seems as if he believes the Bantu philosophy has an a priori origin; that it is some kind of essence build into the Bantu people by birth.

"System fetishism" was common at Tempels' time, for example in the field of ethnography. Today, most ethnographers distance themselves from the system thinking of their predecessors. For example, in *Nuer Dilemmas*, Sharon Hutchinson writes that: "Whereas Evans-Pritchard, like many of his contemporaries, was preoccupied during the 1930s and 1940s with issues of 'unity,' 'equilibrium,' and 'order,' viewing culture as something shared and ethnography as the compilation of those shared elements, this book concentrates on evolving points of confusion among the Nuer—and thus on what was not fully shared by them."[24]

The method Tempels uses to establish his system of Bantu philosophy is problematic as well. He describes the method as a long and tedious grouping and searching, conceiving an idea and soon afterwards rejecting it, the endeavor finally resulting in well-defined ideas fitting into a logical system.[25] I believe that the end result of this process, the well-defined ideas that fit into a logical system—in other words the Bantu philosophy—are to a great extent a construction of Tempels' own mind and a result of his "obsession" with logical systems. It is Tempels who identifies what *he* thinks are the fundamental ideas of the Bantu, and it is *he* who uses these ideas to construct a logical system in which all the different elements of the system fit neatly together.

Tempels explains that after he has described the Bantu philosophy, he will present examples from native ways of expressing themselves, and of behavior, which support his thesis. He claims that: "If the application of this view of Bantu philosophy yield a satisfactory explanation of observed facts, we may find therein a proof of the validity, even of the exactitude of our assumptions."[26] However, the idea that a theory can be proven valid through verification, while unchallenged in Tempels' time, is indefensible as unfolded below.

The idea of proof through verification was efficiently criticized by Karl Popper in the 1960s in his book *Conjectures and Refutations: The Growth of Scientific Knowledge* (1963). Popper explains that as a young man, he was fascinated by Einstein's theory of relativity, Marx's theory of history, Freud's psychoanalysis, and Adler's individual psychology. However, as time went on, he became increasingly dissatisfied with the Marxist theory of history, and also with the theories of Freud and Adler. In fact, he began to feel that these theories "though posing as science, had in fact more in common with primitive myths than with science; that they resembled astrology rather than astronomy."[27] Additionally, Popper explains:

> I found that those of my friends who were admirers of Marx, Freud, and Adler, were impressed by a number of points common to these theories, and especially by their apparent explanatory power. These theories [like Tempels' theory of the Bantu philosophy] appear to be able to explain practically everything that happened within the fields to which they referred. The study of any of them seemed to have the

effect of an intellectual conversion or revelation, opening your eyes to a new truth hidden from those not yet initiated. Once your eyes were thus opened you saw confirmed instances everywhere: the world was full of verifications of the theory. Whatever happened always confirmed it.[28]

As Popper correctly states, almost any theory can be verified if confirmation is what we look for.[29] Against this background, he argues that "[e]very genuine test of a theory is an attempt to falsify it, or to refute it."[30] Furthermore, he explains that if a theory cannot be proven wrong by any imaginable event, it is not scientific. Counterintuitively, Popper clarifies that it does not prove a theory stronger if it is irrefutable; rather, the opposite.[31] Popper's critique of Marxist theory of history, Freud's psychoanalysis, and Adler's individual psychology is exactly that they—unlike Einstein's theory of relativity—are impossible to falsify, and thus non-scientific.

I have a similar critique of Tempels' *Bantu Philosophy*. Firstly, Temples simply does not prove the validity of his theory of the Bantu philosophy by providing empirical examples that confirm it. As Popper tells us, a theory cannot be proven valid by being confirmed by empirical examples. Furthermore, and even more problematic: it seems impossible to falsify Tempels' theory, at least if one accepts the following premises found in Tempels' book:

1. The Bantu are not able to give a systematic exposition of their own philosophy; it is Europeans who will tell them what their inmost concept of being is;
2. The Bantu philosophy can manifest itself in apparently contradictory practices.

The first premise implies that if an individual of the Bantu peoples claims that the Bantu philosophy does not correspond to his or her ideas, Tempels could reply that the claim is due to ignorance: that this individual does not know what his or her inmost concept of being is. As a consequence of the second premise, it is impossible to point to any practice which would falsify Tempels' interpretations. At the very least, Tempels gives us no clue as to what kind of behavior could possibly be sufficient for falsification.

ETHNOPHILOSOPHY AS A TREND IN AFRICAN PHILOSOPHY

The word "ethnophilosophy" was coined by the Beninese philosopher Paulin J. Hountondji, and first appeared in the following passage from his article "Comments on Contemporary African Philosophy":

> *La Philosophie Bantoue*, written by this Belgian missionary [Tempels], still passes for a classic of "African Philosophy" in some eyes. From our

point of view, it appears more like a work of ethnology which has philosophic pretensions, or, more simply, if one may be excused the neologism, a work of ethnophilosophy.[32]

Hountondji emphasizes the profound influence of Tempels' book on African philosophy, "*La Philosophie Bantoue* did indeed prepare the way for all later attempts to reconstruct a particular *Weltanschauung*, a specific world view which is supposedly shared by all Africans, beyond the influence of history and change, and, in addition, *philosophic*."[33] In fact he claims that until the time of publication of his own article (1970), ethnophilosophy had been, owing to Tempels' influence, the only kind of African philosophy.[34] To Hountondji, this was problematic, because the ethnophilosophers were deceiving themselves: "They thought to reproduce pre-existing philosophical themes when they were in fact creating."[35] For Hountondji, this had the severe consequence that African philosophy had been "*imaginary research* [emphasis mine] after a collective philosophy, which might be unchangeable, shared by all Africans, even if it existed in an unconscious form."[36]

As explained by Barry Hallen, and reflected in the quotes from Hountondji above, "ethnophilosophy began its conceptual life as an appellation used to stigmatize what was said to be a distinctively dysfunctional form of African philosophy."[37] Hountondji categorizes Tempels, Alexis Kagame, André Makarakiza, Francois-Marie Lufuluabo, Vincent Mulago, Jean-Calvin Bahoken, Basile-Juleat Fouda, and William Abraham as ethnophilosophers.[38] According to Ochieng'-Odhiambo, John Mbiti, Robin Horton, and Marcel Griaule also belong to this group.[39] According to Didier N. Kaphagawani, Tempels, Kagame, and Mbiti are the chief representatives of the ethnophilosophical trend in African philosophy,[40] although this is a topic for discussion elsewhere.[41]

According to Hountondji, ethnophilosophy is nothing but a myth; and this remains one of the severest critiques of ethnophilosophy ever presented. Hountondji writes that the weakness of the ethnophilosophers was that they did not "realize the *philosophic form* of their own arguments mythically, in the guise of a collective philosophy."[42] In Hountondji's view: "To do away with that myth once and for all, and free our conceptual horizon for a real theoretical discussion, is the task which falls to African scientists and philosophers today."[43]

Hountondji was also the first to present another very significant critique of ethnophilosophy, namely, that this kind of philosophy does not serve Africans well. One reason is that ethnophilosophy has been closely linked to the colonial project, as evident in Tempels' case. Hountondji writes: "The humanist thinker [Tempels] unmasks himself as a real preserver of the colonial order [. . .] and his hazy abstractions are seen to be very concrete ways of supporting an in itself concrete policy: the maintenance of imperialist domination."[44] I agree. The primary reason why

Tempels described the Bantu philosophy was to help the Europeans to greater success in governing, civilizing, and educating the Bantu people. Thus Ernest Wamba-dia-Wamba has written that "ethnophilosophy is a philosophy of and for the dominated Africa."[45] Hountondji even refers to the ideological myth of a collective African philosophy as "a new and simply reevaluated version of the 'primitive mentality' of Lévy-Bruhl."[46]

The idea that Africans had a primitive mentality was the shameful legacy of a long and racist history. African individuals have exactly the same capacity for critical individual thinking as others, and just as it does not make sense to talk about a unified philosophy of Europeans, Americans, Asians, etc., it does not make sense to talk about a unified philosophy of Africans. The ideas of individuals certainly can be shaped by their environment, but this does not mean that individuals cannot create and develop their own ideas. Furthermore, it is beyond question that individuals who share the same group identity do not always share the same ideas. For example, not all Africans share the same *ubuntu* ideas, which will be unfolded in the next chapter where I delve into the diversity and development of *ubuntu* ideas.

NOTES

1. Andrew Valls, ed., *Race and Racism in Modern Philosophy* (New York: Cornell University Press, 2005).
2. David Hume, *Essays and Treatises on Several Subjects*, vol. 1 (London: A. Millar, 1758), 125.
3. Placide Tempels, *Bantu Philosophy*, trans. Colin King (Paris: Présence Africaine, 1959), 16.
4. Ibid., 14.
5. Ibid.
6. Ibid., 15.
7. Ibid.
8. Ibid., 18.
9. Ibid., 15, 60.
10. Ibid., 60.
11. Ibid.
12. Ibid., 15.
13. Ibid., 25.
14. Ibid., 34.
15. Ibid.
16. Ibid., 35.
17. Ibid., 32.
18. Ibid., 41.
19. Ibid., 42.
20. Ibid., 50.
21. Ibid.
22. Ibid.
23. Ibid., 24.
24. Sharon E. Hutchinson, *Nuer Dilemmas: Coping with Money, War, and the State* (Berkeley: University of California Press, 1996), 28.
25. Tempels, *Bantu Philosophy*, 28.

26. Ibid., 29.
27. Karl Popper, *Conjectures and Refutations: The Growth of Scientific Knowledge* (London: Routledge, 1963), 45.
28. Ibid.
29. Ibid., 47.
30. Ibid., 48.
31. Ibid.
32. Paulin J. Hountondji, "Comments on Contemporary African Philosophy," *Diogenes* 71 (1970): 111.
33. Ibid., 112.
34. Ibid., 117. I do not agree with Hountondji that ethnophilosophy was the only kind of African philosophy until 1970. As noted in the introduction, the nationalist-ideological trend developed as early as the late 1950s.
35. Ibid., 117.
36. Ibid.
37. Barry Hallen, "'Ethnophilosophy' Redefined?" *Thought and Practice: A Journal of the Philosophical Association of Kenya* 2, no. 1 (2010): 83.
38. Hountondji, "Comments on Contemporary African Philosophy," 127.
39. Ochieng'-Odhiambo, *Trends and Issues*, 40–64.
40. Didier N. Kaphagawani, "What is African Philosophy?" in *The African Philosophy Reader*, ed. P. H. Coetzee and A. R. J. Roux (London: Routledge, 1998), 89.
41. For example, in the chapter on ethnophilosophy in *Trends and Issues in African Philosophy*, Frederick Ochieng'-Odhiambo focusses on Tempels, Mbiti and Horton, and only writes about Kagame's work in a section on "Other Ethnophilosophers and General Critiques." See page 64 ff.
42. Hountondji, "Comments on Contemporary African Philosophy," 118.
43. Ibid., 127.
44. Ibid., 116.
45. Ernest Wamba-dia-Wamba, "Philosophy and African Intellectuals: Mimesis of Western Classicism. Ethnophilosophical Romanticism or African Self-Mastery," *Quest* 5, no. 1 (1991): 10.
46. Hountondji, "Comments on Contemporary African Philosophy," 125.

SIX

The Diversity and Development of *Ubuntu* Ideas[1]

The justified critique of ethnophilosophy by Hountondji and others led to the increasing individualization of African philosophy, with the emergence of trends such as philosophic sagacity and professional philosophy. In the first of these trends, African philosophy is identified with the philosophical thought of individual African sages, whereas in the second it is identified with the thought of professionally trained African philosophers.[2] In both cases, there is a focus on the critical thinking of *individual* Africans.

I believe it is possible to have meaningful collective approaches to African philosophy which are not mythical in nature. In fact, my research on *ubuntu* and the TRC demonstrates one such approach, and it is radically different from that taken by Tempels, as it gives due consideration to differences, historical developments, and social contexts. As shown in the previous chapter, Tempels takes for granted the existence of a collectively shared and static philosophy. His starting point is to formulate a theory about the constitution of this philosophy, whereupon he presents empirical data in an attempt to verify his theory. My starting point, on the other hand, has been to conduct empirical investigations by means of qualitative interviews and historical text investigations in order to explore whether ideas are collectively shared and static, always being open to the possibility that this may not be the case. Subsequently, I reflect theoretically on my findings using ideas from Praeg, Nietzsche, etc. in an attempt to understand what I have found.

My discourse on African philosophy is *collective* in the sense that I—like the ethnophilosopers—do not focus on any individual in particular, but explore how *ubuntu* is understood by South Africans. What my findings highlight is that though some South Africans share an understanding of *ubuntu*, there is a considerable diversity of *ubuntu* ideas among them. In fact, the diversity may be even greater than reflected in my research, as there may be several interpretations of *ubuntu* which I have not been able to identify. Thus, it is evident that *ubuntu* has multiple meanings, as emphasized by Wilson:

> *Ubuntu* should be recognized for what it is: an ideological concept with multiple meanings which conjoins human rights, restorative justice, reconciliation and nation building within the populist language of pan-Africanism.[3]

The multiple meanings of *ubuntu* imply that if people do not explain exactly what they mean by the word—and often they do not—it may be quite unclear what they are talking about. Certainly, this adds a thick layer of vagueness to much of the *ubuntu* talk in post-apartheid South Africa. This said, I will now move on to present my findings on the differing interpretations of *ubuntu*.

UBUNTU AS A MORAL QUALITY

My research demonstrates that, according to quite a number of South Africans, *ubuntu* is a moral quality in a person. To some, this moral quality is so positive that the very possession of it is praiseworthy. Tutu writes:

> *Ubuntu* is very difficult to render into a Western language. It speaks of the very essence of being human. When we want to give high praise to someone we say, "*Yu, u nobuntu*"; "Hey, he or she has *ubuntu*." This means that they are generous, hospitable, friendly, caring, and compassionate.[4]

Bhengu, the former member of parliament I mentioned in chapter two, also describes *ubuntu* as a kind of "soul force":

> Gandhi gave India the spiritual concept of "soul force" (*satyagraha*), a capacity to sustain and transcend physical discomfort in a triumph of concentration and restraint. Why should we Africans not give South Africa that "soul force" (*ubuntu*)?[5]

Furthermore, during an interview, Bhengu told me that *ubuntu* is a kind of divine element which stops human beings from doing something wrong:

> There is God in a human being. That is why even at your home when your parents are not around, and you try to steal, something says to you: "Ah . . . don't, don't!" And then sometimes you say: "Hey . . . I mustn't." Nyerere refers to it as a spark saying: "Please don't do." That is *ubuntu*.[6]

Gobodo-Madikizela, the former TRC committee member quoted in chapter four, explained that empathy is an essential aspect of *ubuntu*. To elaborate on what she meant, she offered an example:

> Its essence is about the capacity for empathy with another person. You see, that is the essence of *ubuntu*: that capacity which I think is something we ought to have as human beings, and which is present in all of us, that capacity to connect with another human being, to be touched, to be moved by another human being. That is *ubuntu*. If I walk down the street, and I see someone . . . I can see something in his face that says that this person is going through a difficult moment. I do not have time but I turn to him and say: "How are you today?" That is *ubuntu* because I am connecting to how he seems to be feeling at the moment, and I am reaching out, and I am acknowledging that I see his pain and want to leave him with some kindness as I walk past him.[7]

Another example of how the moral quality *ubuntu* can be expressed in behavior is provided by Cecil Mlanjeni, one of the many victims of gross human rights violations who gave testimony to the TRC. He said:

> What I can do to explain *ubuntu* to you is to give an example: I meet you. I don't know you. Maybe you are stuck. Sometimes you don't even know the road. I have to show you the road or otherwise take you to where you want to go, and I have to take care of you in such manner that you feel comfortable. Maybe you are lost in an area that you don't know; for instance you are in our areas. You don't know our areas but we come to you and assist you and secure you, so that you feel comfortable. If I don't have transport to take you somewhere, then I have to ask somebody to take you. That is the soul of *ubuntu* in practice.[8]

Some South Africans depict *ubuntu* as a rather complex, multi-faceted quality. Tutu writes, for example, that if persons possess *ubuntu* it means that they are "generous, hospitable, friendly, caring and compassionate."[9] One aspect of the moral quality of *ubuntu* is often held to be the capacity to forgive, as we have already seen in chapter four. Before quoting Cecile Hlokofa on *ubuntu* and forgiveness, I want to draw attention to the fact that she suffered greatly under apartheid and that one might perhaps not expect her to be open to the idea of forgiveness. However, she saw forgiveness as an ideal. Below, Hlokofa speaks about her testimony to the TRC:

> Gade: Could you tell me a little about what human rights violations it was that formed the background for your statement to the TRC?
>
> Hlokofa: The statement was about the way my husband was killed and my arm was broken in Crossroads [township area near Cape Town International Airport]. It was early in the morning on a Sunday when the loud hailer said that all the men should attend a meeting. The people went there only to listen to what it was about. That was when they were attacked. They were beaten and shot at, so everybody was

running around; it was a hell of a chaos. My husband was shot dead. Everyone was running around the area, and I was caught by these people. I was beaten, and they broke my arm. Most people died in that incident, and we don't know why people were called in.[10]

After retelling the incident, Hlokofa said:

> I can describe *ubuntu* in the manner of an example, perhaps. If you did something wrong to me, let me not have a "Drat on you!" I must just give you an apology even though you do not come to me and give an apology. Even if you did a nasty thing, I have to be calm to you and be apologetic. So that is how I can explain *ubuntu*.[11]

Sindiswa Nunu from the Khulumani support group translated what Hlokofa said in isiXhosa into English, and just after the statement, she elaborated on what Hlokofa meant: "You have to forgive! Whatever you did to me, let me forgive you—that would be *ubuntu*." Speaking about Nelson Mandela, former TRC commissioner Mgojo, whom I also quoted in chapter four, said:

> Mgojo: In most places, you can't have a person who suffered like that, like Mandela, doing that thing [forgiving former enemies]. But the *ubuntu* was pushing him. If you have this [*ubuntu*], then you must forgive, but not forget. You must forgive, but not forget because if you forget, you will repeat the same thing. You see?
>
> Gade: Just for me to understand it. . . . It is a very interesting link you make between *ubuntu* and forgiveness. So you think that if people have *ubuntu*, then they are likely. . .
>
> Mgojo: They *must* forgive, especially when people are religious people. How many times does God forgive us? In fact we should be punished every time by God, but God forgives us because of this godliness, which has to boost what we call *ubuntu*.[12]

Former TRC commissioner Ntsebeza, likewise quoted in chapter four, connected *ubuntu* and forgiveness through another example:

> Ntsebeza: So we investigated [the killing of the Gugulethu Seven] and everything that I just told you—the planning, the heading from Pretoria, the Vlakplass involvement, Eugene de Kock's involvement—all of that came out in an investigation, a special investigation that was conducted by the Western Cape branch of the Investigative Unit. So what had been perpetuated from 1986 in the media and South African history as having been a terrorist attack that was foiled by the police was shown in fact for what it really was. And it brought a lot of trauma to the victims, to those mothers, because for all those years until 1997–1998 when we exposed the evil of what had happened, how their children had been lured into a death trap. . . [Sentence not finished].
>
> When we revealed all that, the mothers started to be more traumatized, but in some very strange way they were able to relate to the revelation of the truth. They had this catharsis that was brought about

by the knowledge that their sons were actually murdered, rather than being killed as they were attempting [to conduct a terrorist attack]. So there was a shift in the morality of the kill, of the event.

Now when one of the killers applied for amnesty, we made an arrangement after he had testified for him to meet a group of the mothers. We arranged a private session. It was remarkable what happened there! This guy was open; he did not pretend to justify, he was asking for them to find it in their hearts to forgive him if they could ever do that. And one of the mothers was very remarkable in the way that she dealt with this. She said: "Look, there is nothing we can do now about the people who died. But one thing that causes us to feel released and liberated is the fact that you are sitting here. You are somebody and some other woman's child. You are sitting here, and you are telling how you slaughtered our children, and the mere fact that you have now found the courage to come and talk to us. . . . Whatever happens to your amnesty application, we have forgiven you." This is a very dramatic example.

Gade: So you think that the mother who was able to forgive had *ubuntu*?

Ntsebeza: Yes.[13]

UBUNTU AND INTERCONNECTEDNESS

Above, *ubuntu* is described as a moral quality. However, as previously emphasized, there have been many different interpretations of what *ubuntu* is. Some South Africans have defined *ubuntu* as a philosophy, an ethic, African humanism, or as a worldview, as can be illustrated by the following quotations:

> *Ubuntu* is a philosophy that could assist in rebuilding within and amongst different communities.[14]

> It [*ubuntu*] is a social ethic, a unifying vision enshrined in the Zulu maxim *umuntu ngumuntu ngabanye* ("one is a person through others").[15]

> That healthy atmosphere also emanated from the authentic African humanism (*ubuntu*) that pervaded the college.[16]

> *Ubuntu* stresses the importance of community, solidarity, caring, and sharing. This worldview [*ubuntu*] advocates a profound sense of interdependence and emphasizes that our true human potential can only be realized in partnership with others.[17]

Frequently, people do not go into detail about the nature of the philosophy, the ethic, the African humanism, or the worldview that they define as *ubuntu*. But when further explanations are offered, it usually becomes clear that *ubuntu* is understood as a phenomenon that connects persons to one another. For example, Mangosuthu Buthelezi, the leader of Inkatha Freedom Party, has told me that he believes *ubuntu* can best be translated as "humanism," and that *ubuntu* is related to interconnectedness:

> *Ubuntu* is that I am what I am because of you. President Kaunda of Zambia wrote a book on [African] humanism. It is the nearest English equivalent to that. I think that "humanism" is the nearest translation of what *ubuntu* is.[18]

Finca, the former TRC commissioner quoted in chapter four, elaborated in greater detail the idea that *ubuntu* is about interconnectedness. He emphasized that a person is not an island, as the well-being of the person depends on the well-being of the community:

> You are what you are because of other people. We don't live in isolation, we live in a community. That sense of community is what makes you who you are, and if that community becomes broken, then you yourselves also become broken. And the restoration of that community, the healing of that community, cannot happen unless you contribute to the healing of it in a broader sense. Basically that is it. *Ubuntu* is that I am because of others, in relationship with others. I am not an island of myself, I am part of the community, I am part of the greater group.[19]

Mgojo also described *ubuntu* as something that has to do with interconnectedness, and he made a link between *ubuntu* and the idea of collective shame:

> With us it is you, family, clan and nation. The tying factor is called *ubuntu*. What injures me is injuring you, what injures us is injuring our clan, what is injuring our clan is injuring the whole community and the nation. That is *ubuntu*. You cannot live as an individual. That is why, when you are doing a wrong thing, you are putting shame on the whole group.[20]

Tutu, speaking likewise in terms of interconnectedness, refers to *ubuntu* as a phenomenon that implies that the humanity of the perpetrator of the atrocities of apartheid itself became caught up in the humanity of his victim:

> *Ubuntu* means that in a real sense even the supporters of apartheid were victims of the vicious system which they implemented and which they supported so enthusiastically. Our humanity was intertwined. The humanity of the perpetrator of apartheid's atrocities was caught up and bound up in that of his victim whether he liked it or not. In the process of dehumanizing another, in inflicting untold harm and suffering, the perpetrator was inexorably being dehumanized as well.[21]

In this connection, Finca explained that crime is a bad thing above all because it has negative effects on the harmony of the community, and that according to *ubuntu* it is more important to restore communal harmony than to secure punishment:

> Instead of pursuing punishment, you are more interested in restoring relationships. That is fundamental to *ubuntu* because *ubuntu* does not focus on what has been done to you, *ubuntu* focuses on how we can be restored together as a community, so that we can heal together. *Ubuntu* does not only concentrate on the pain that has been caused to me, but also recognizes the damage that has been done to you. In the course of what you are doing to me, you are also hurting yourself.[22]

Finca added:

> *Ubuntu* wants that in the process of me being restored, you must also be restored, because we can only be fully human when we are human together. You must heal and I must assist you to heal, as much as I must heal and you must assist me to heal.

THE CONCEPT OF A PERSON

The concept of a person (*umuntu* in the Nguni languages) is of central importance to the understanding of *ubuntu*. As we have seen, some claim that *ubuntu* is a moral quality in a person, while others define it as a phenomenon—for instance a philosophy, an ethic, African humanism, or a worldview—according to which persons are interconnected. The moral quality of a person is, logically speaking, something that only a person can possess, and you have to be a person to be part of the interconnectedness of persons.

All Members of Homo Sapiens are Persons

According to some, but not all, South Africans, all members of the species Homo sapiens count as persons. This inclusive conception of a person is, for example, presented by Bhengu in his book *Ubuntu: The Essence of Democracy*:

> A primary characteristic of African "being" is its inclusiveness. African theology declares that *umuntu* is a dynamic concept: it means *all* humans not only African humans.[23]

In an interview, Bhekithemba Mchunu, a prince of the Zulu royal house and an *induna* (adviser) of traditional leaders in KwaZulu Natal, also underscored that "we are all *abantu*" [plural of *umuntu*, meaning "persons"], and he even specified that "it [the term *umuntu*] does not only refer to somebody who is black, somebody who has undergone rituals."[24]

Only Blacks are Persons

Some Africans claim that not all members of Homo sapiens are persons. Samkange and Samkange wrote in 1980 (as discussed in chapter two) that "When one sees two people, one white and the other black, coming along, we say: *Hona munhu uyo ari kufamba murungu* [chiShona], or in isiNdebele [one of the Nguni languages], *Nanguyana umuntu ohamba lo mlungu.*"[25] This means: "There is a *munhu/umuntu* [person] walking with a white man." The Samkanges explain why people say this:

> Now, is there a sense in which we can say that a white man lacks something which we always identify in an African? Yes, black Americans, for instance, identify something they call "soul" as being almost exclusively among black folk. What is this thing they call soul? It is indefinable, yet identifiable among black people.[26]

The idea that only blacks are persons is also mentioned in other sources. Aninka Claassens worked as a TRAC (Transvaal Rural Action Committee) fieldworker in South African rural areas, and in 1986 she published a short article in the journal *The Black Sash*. Here she explained how black South Africans, in her experience, understood the concept of *abantu*:

> *Abantu* sometimes has another meaning, which is "black people," white people not being included. It is necessary to specify who is in the world before one can continue to call everyone there *abantu*. Otherwise when you mention that one of these *abantu* is called Oliver Twist people look skeptical—*abantu* don't have names like that. It's sad really to have to say *abantu nabaMhlope*, "people and whites," particularly when the word *abantu* is a personification of the quality *ubuntu*—meaning human behavior, compassion, humanity. It is however not all that surprising—whites have used the word "Bantu" to mean "Black people" and there has been a terrible shortage of *ubuntu* in white people's behavior towards black.[27]

Some Black South Africans have also elaborated on the view that only blacks are *abantu*. In a speech on the proud legacy of Mandela held at a symposium organized by the Department of Education in Port Elizabeth, Fred Khumalo, an award-winning columnist, said:

> Now, I was born and bred in KwaZulu Natal, grew up in a tiny township called Mpumalanga in the midlands area. Thanks to the tales of valor that we listened to from our grandmothers, all the heroes that we were told of were Zulu. My world view revolved around *abantu* (human beings, meaning black people) and *abelungu* (whites). There was no rancor in our attitudes towards whites, but they were simply not *abantu*. My world view—and I suppose that I speak on behalf of many of my peers—was that narrow.[28]

When I interviewed Buthelezi, he referred to the idea that only blacks are persons as a confusion caused by the apartheid regime:

You know what, that [idea] was caused by the apartheid regime. Because the apartheid regime—at one time they called us "Bantu" as if it refers to black people only. The word *abantu* in fact refers to people [all members of *Homo sapiens*]. It was an official designation of black people that one was *abantu*, which is a plural of *umuntu*. It was awkward because if you were a black sergeant in the police, they would not say "sergeant so and so," they would say "Bantu sergeant so and so." That confusion was caused by that.[29]

A Person Through Ritual Incorporation

In *African Philosophy Through Ubuntu*, Ramose explains that in traditional African thought, a member of Homo sapiens is not a person by birth, but is incorporated into personhood:

> In order to be a person the human individual must, according to traditional African thought, go through various community prescribed stages, and be part of certain ceremonies and rituals. Only at the completion of all prescribed stages does the human individual acquire the status of a person. Prior to this the individual is regarded as "it" to show that he or she is not yet incorporated into the body of persons. In traditional African thought personhood is, therefore, acquired and not merely established by virtue of the fact of being human.[30]

To support this interpretation, Ramose refers to the work of Ifeanyi A. Menkiti, an acknowledged Nigerian philosopher. In the famous article, "Persons and Community in African Traditional Thought," Menkiti explains that:

> Without incorporation into this or that community, individuals are considered to be mere danglers to whom the description "person" does not fully apply. For personhood is something which has to be achieved, and it is not given simply because one is born of human seed.[31]

In contemporary African philosophy, the conception of a person described by Ramose is sometimes referred to as "the normative conception of a person."[32] Wiredu offers insight as to how this conception has developed in the literature:

> A person is not just a certain biological entity with a certain psychophysical endowment, but, rather, a being of this kind who has shown a basic willingness and ability to fulfill his or her obligations in the community. Personhood, on this showing, is something of an achievement. It is only comparatively recently that attention has been called, in contemporary African philosophy, to this normative character of the traditional African concept of a person. In anthropology, however, Meyer Fortes, in the 1940s, noted (1987[33]) the normative dimensions of the concept of a person among the Tallensi of Northern Ghana and other African peoples. In contemporary African philosophy the *locus classicus*

of the normative conception of a person is Ifeanyi Menkiti's "Persons and Community in African Traditional Thought" (1984).[34]

The Behavior of a Person

Some individuals from the Bantu group also believe that members of Homo sapiens can demonstrate that they are *not* persons by the way they behave. This belief, like the previous one, represents a normative conception of a person: a conception according to which the status of being a person depends on a normative evaluation of behavior. As Buthelezi has said, "If a person behaves in a way which is not consonant with expected human behavior, then we say that he is no longer *umuntu* because he has not got *ubuntu*. So you sort of classify him as an animal."[35] In line with this statement, Bhengu explained:

> The moment you go outside the boundaries of *ubuntu*, you actually begin to be labeled an animal [by the community]—*kintu* [animal] as opposed to *ubuntu*. Once you are at this level, even your community, they just reject and repel [you].[36]

Mchunu went into further detail talking about the area in KwaZulu Natal where he is an *induna*:

> Mchunu: He [the murderer or the rapist] is not considered to be a human being *at all* because of the way he is behaving toward other people.
>
> Gade: So that is actually an example where not everybody is considered to be *abantu*?
>
> Mchunu: Exactly, the community will say—they even say it: "You are not a human being. You do not deserve to be with us." They would say that. Even today, such cases do happen. They [the community members] can go to the extent where they kill a person. We have had some cases where a person is stoned, where a person is killed.
>
> Gade: Even today?
>
> Mchunu: Even today, it does happen.
>
> Gade: Because they are not considered to be persons?
>
> Mchunu: In rape cases where a person is found raping somebody, or killing somebody. . . If you are not there as a traditional leader to calm them down, people will take the law into their own hands. They would kill that person for the sake of protecting *ubuntu* because that person has lost humanity. He is no longer a person. He is regarded as an animal, because what he is doing is not accepted.[37]

THE WRITTEN HISTORY OF UBUNTU

We have now seen that there are differing interpretations of *ubuntu*, partly due to differing interpretations of who counts as a person. In the following, I will present a historical analysis of how *ubuntu* has been defined in the written sources. This analysis, which has been conducted by means of the search functions in electronic text databases, demonstrates that some contemporary interpretations of *ubuntu* have deep historical roots, whereas others may have developed in recent years.[38]

Many authors have argued that the written exposition of *ubuntu* is relatively new. Gabriel Setiloane has stated that the term *ubuntu* was first used in South African writing in an address to a conference held in Durban in 1960,[39] and Tom Lodge has explained that *ubuntu* was first given a systematic written exposition in the novels of Jordan Kush Ngubane.[40] Furthermore, Van Binsbergen (as mentioned in chapter one) has stated that to his knowledge the oldest text on *ubuntu* is the Samkanges' *Hunhuims or Ubuntuism: A Zimbabwe Indigenous Political Philosophy*, dating from 1980. I have in fact discovered a number of older texts containing the term *ubuntu*, the oldest dating from 1846.[41] My findings show that prior to 1980, when the term *ubuntu* was used in the political project of the Samkanges (see chapter two), *ubuntu* was most commonly described as "human nature,"[42] "humanity,"[43] and "humanness."[44] In some pre-1980 texts, *ubuntu* is also described as:

- Manhood[45]
- Goodness of nature[46]
- Good moral disposition[47]
- Virtue[48]
- Humaneness[49]
- The sense of common humanity[50]
- True humanity[51]
- True good fellowship and sympathy in joy and in sorrow[52]
- Reverence for human nature[53]
- Essential humanity[54]
- The kindly simple feeling for persons as persons[55]
- Manliness[56]
- Liberality[57]
- A person's own human nature[58]
- Human feeling[59]
- Good disposition[60]
- Good moral nature[61]
- Personhood[62]
- Politeness[63]
- Kindness[64]
- Real humanity[65]

- Humanity (benevolence)[66]
- Personality[67]
- Human kindness[68]
- The characteristic of being truly human[69]
- Greatness of soul[70]
- A feeling of human well-being[71]
- Capacity of social self-sacrifice on behalf of others[72]
- Generosity[73]

Figure 6.1 below is an illustration of how *ubuntu*—according to my findings—has been defined in the written sources during different historical periods.

Ubuntu *as a Quality*

In a number of texts, the term "quality" appears in descriptions of *ubuntu*,[74] and in many of the texts, it is evident that *ubuntu* is considered to be a very positive quality. As shown above, *ubuntu* is, for example, described as "goodness of nature," "good moral disposition," and as "greatness of soul." While some authors simply describe *ubuntu* as a "human quality,"[75] others emphasize that it is a quality connected to a specific group. More specifically, *ubuntu* is described as an "excellent African quality,"[76] a quality among "the admirable qualities of the Bantu,"[77] and "an essentially Native quality."[78] My results also include authors who state that *ubuntu* is a quality that blacks possess and whites lack,[79] as well as one author who explains that: "Initiation is a ladder to humanity (*ubuntu*) and respect."[80] These statements are expressions of the previously mentioned idea that *ubuntu* is something limited to specific groups.

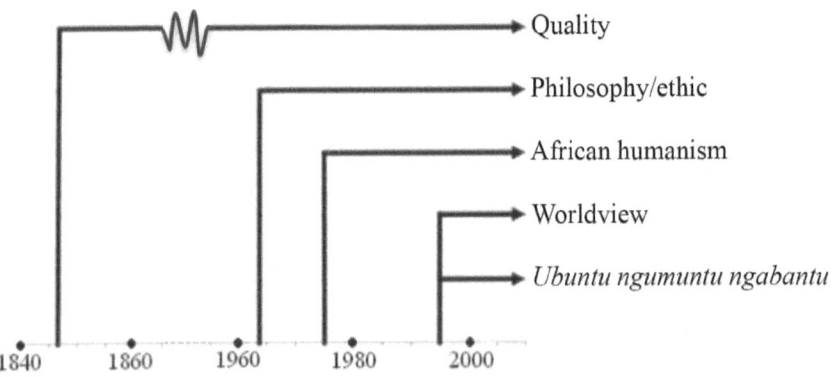

Figure 6.1. Historical overview of *ubuntu*'s definitions in written sources. *Created by the author.*

Right up to the present day, a number of authors continue to characterize *ubuntu* as a positive quality, as we have seen earlier in this chapter. A few additional illustrative quotes:

> Mr Nhlapo was held in very high respect by the black people of the district, and if he and his wife could go to the house of the white headmaster for dinner, then the white headmaster and his wife must be human beings, they must have the quality of *ubuntu*, which is the quality of humaneness, the quality of human beings when they are at their highest and best.[81]

> Africans are a people whose identity is founded on *ubuntu*. Meaning "personhood," *ubuntu* expresses a unique quality about a person which elevates him or her to a plane near to godliness.[82]

> *Ubuntu* is an African word that speaks of humanity and its goodness. The word has the meaning of being human, of being generous and gracious. You still find this in African society, and this concept is shared with the West when people come to visit. It is the sense of human grace and honor that prevailed in Africa even prior to the arrival of the missionaries.[83]

Ubuntu *as a Philosophy or an Ethic*

My findings suggest that from the 1960s onwards, a new idea began to appear in writing, namely that *ubuntu* is closely connected to, or even *is*, a philosophy or an ethic. In *An African Explains Apartheid* (1963), Jordan Kush Ngubane characterizes *ubuntu* as a philosophy of life, writing:

> Supreme virtue lay in being humane, in accepting the human being as part of yourself, with a right to be denied nothing that you possessed. It was inhuman to drive the hungry stranger from your door, for your neighbor's sorrow was yours. This code constituted a philosophy of life, and the great Sutu-nguni family (Bantu has political connotations that the Africans resent) called it, significantly, *ubuntu* or *botho*—pronounced *butu*—the practice of being humane.[84]

In *Conflicts of Minds* (1979), Ngubane also defines *ubuntu* as "the philosophy which the African experience translates into action,"[85] and in *African Religions: A Symposium* (1977), Newell Snow Booth explains: "The concept of *ubuntu*, the recognition of a person as a person, is basic to the ethics of all the southern Bantu."[86] Furthermore, in *Black Villagers in an Industrial Society* (1980), Philip Mayer relates that: "the occurrence of the same ideas through the whole spectrum of Blacks from the least educated, leaves no doubt that the main source was in African philosophy, in the concept of *ubuntu* which is associated with kindness, gentleness, humility, respect and love."[87] Later, during the transformation of society in South Africa in the 1990s, expressions such as "*ubuntu* philosophy" or "ethic of *ubuntu*" became common. A couple of illustrative quotes:

> In *ubuntu* philosophy a human being in the world of the living must be *umuntu* in order to give a response to the challenge of the fundamental instability of being.[88]

> In another discussion, on Luke's version of the Lord's Prayer, the BCC noted that they might not have much in the way of money or food, but they were able to survive because they "had God." In a bourgeois setting, one would expect this to mean something like a spiritual or personal sense of support or comfort, but here it meant that "Maybe God has already talked to a neighbor who will have a plate ready for me when I come" (not an unusual occurrence in African society under the ethic of *ubuntu*).[89]

Since the 2000s, it has been very common to identify *ubuntu* as a philosophy or an ethic, as in the examples below:

> *Ubuntu* is a philosophy that promotes the common good of society and includes humanness as an essential element of human growth.[90]

> *Ubuntu* is a philosophy that could assist in rebuilding within and amongst different communities.[91]

> *Ubuntu* is an ethic that developed in a context of essential interdependence and severe need.[92]

> *Ubuntu* is an ethic, or ideology, based on an African worldview and an interdependent anthropology.[93]

Ubuntu *as African Humanism*

I have found three texts from the 1970s which describe *ubuntu* as "African humanism."[94] Similar descriptions are found in texts from later decades:

> As Buthelezi has noted: "There is a great deal in me which is formed by my deep affinity to African humanism—*Ubuntu/Botho*—and I find many aspects of Western industrialized societies offensive to my humanist tendencies."[95]

> *Ubuntu*, which she [Chikanda] sees as African Humanism, involves aid-giving, sympathy, care, sensitivity to the needs of others, respect, consideration, patience, and kindness.[96]

> *Ubuntu*, as this African humanism is termed in the South African context, is part of a spiritual reconstruction aimed at filling the void of meaning and value left by the dismantled apartheid regime.[97]

Ubuntu *as a Worldview*

In the 1990s, some authors also began to use the expression "worldview" to describe what *ubuntu* is. In *No Future without Forgiveness*, Tutu wrote that *ubuntu* is a worldview consistent with the TRC amnesty (he has made similar claims in other contexts—see, for example, the quote from Tutu in the beginning of chapter four):

> I want to conclude this chapter [entitled "Nuremberg or National Amnesia? A Third Way?"] by pointing out that this third way of conditional amnesty was consistent with a central feature of the African *Weltanschauung* (or worldview)—that we know as *ubuntu* in Nguni group of languages[98]

Since 2000, *ubuntu* has frequently been described as a worldview. I have already explained that Krog refers to *ubuntu* as a worldview in the 2008 article where she argues that *ubuntu* was the essence and foundation of the TRC process, and thus she uses an interpretation of *ubuntu* which has only a short history in the written sources. Other examples from the 2000s are:

> Confronting the past was very much about providing a new model, a new moral basis for individuals and institutions but especially for the *nation*. While the rhetoric of healing [within the South African Truth and Reconciliation Commission] implied restoration, this was not restoration of the old order, apartheid, but rather of humanity and human dignity. If any old order was being appealed to in the ceremony itself, it was a version of the African humanist philosophy or worldview of *ubuntu*.[99]

> Johann B. writes of the importance of *ubuntu* as a tool to reduce racist attitudes: "If all people abide by and live out the worldview of *ubuntu* which is a reference to the basic values of humanness, love, intense caring and sharing, respect and compassion, South Africa and the whole global world would be freed of all forms of racism.[100]

Umuntu ngumuntu ngabantu

Starting in the 1990s, the Nguni proverb *umuntu ngumuntu ngabantu*, often translated "A person is a person through other persons," has also been used to describe what *ubuntu* is. I list here some illustrative quotations:

> it is worth recalling that humanism also has distinct South African lineages, inasmuch as the Nguni term *ubuntu* refers to the fact that "people are people through other people," (or in Zulu, *umuntu ngumuntu ngabantu*), a principle often invoked by African humanists in South Africa in some way or other.[101]

> *Ubuntu* is short for an isiXhosa proverb in Southern Africa. It comes from *umuntu ngumuntu ngabantu*: a person is a person through their relationship to others.[102]

> *Ubuntu* is an African word that, literally translated, means "people are people through other people."[103]

Towards the end of the 1990s and during the 2000s, some authors mentioned slightly different proverbs in relation to *ubuntu*. An example is:

> Beyond starvation and the tribal atrocities you see in the news of Africa, South Africa's unique gift to the world may well be the spirit of *ubuntu*. In Nelson Mandala's tribal language (Xhosa), one of eleven official languages in South Africa, "Ubuntu ngumntu ngabanye abantu" is roughly translated as "a person is (can only be) a person through other persons."[104]

When *ubuntu* was linked to the proverb *umuntu ngumuntu ngabantu* in the 1990s, it was underscored that *ubuntu* is about interconnectedness. In the context of the post-apartheid reconciliation policy, *ubuntu* thus became a highly useful political tool, and it developed into an ethic for nation building that emphasized the interconnectedness of all South Africans in a fragmented society. Furthermore, the emphasis on *ubuntu* as being about interconnectedness meant that *ubuntu* could become a political counter-ideology to the segregation ideology of the apartheid regime. Thus, the political use of *ubuntu* highlighted the difference between the ANC government and the previous apartheid government. In the next chapter, I go deeper into the political dimensions of *ubuntu*. My point of departure is to revisit the call for a return to *ubuntu*, first discussed in chapter two.

NOTES

1. This chapter includes material from my articles: Christian B. N. Gade, "The Historical Development of the Written Discourses on Ubuntu," *South African Journal of Philosophy* 30, no. 3 (2011); Christian B. N. Gade, "What is *Ubuntu*? Different Interpretations among South Africans of African Descent," *South African Journal of Philosophy* 31, no. 3 (2012): 484–503.

2. See Henry Odera Oruka, *Trends in Contemporary African Philosophy* (Nairobi: Shirikon Publishers, 1990); Frederick Ochieng'-Odhiambo, *Trends and Issues in African Philosophy* (New York: Peter Lang, 2010).

3. Richard A. Wilson, *The Politics of Truth and Reconciliation in South Africa: Legitimizing the Post-Apartheid State* (Cambridge: Cambridge University Press, 2001), 13.

4. Desmond Tutu, *No Future Without Forgiveness* (London: Rider, 1999), 34.

5. Mfuniselwa J. Bhengu, *Ubuntu: The Essence of Democracy* (Cape Town: Novalis Press, 1996), 19.

6. Mfuniselwa John Bhengu, interviewed by author, Dec. 17, 2009, Durban.

7. Gobodo-Madikizela, interview.

8. Cecil Mlanjeni, interviewed by author, Nov. 5, 2008, Cape Town.

9. Desmond Tutu, *No Future Without Forgiveness* (London: Rider, 1999), 34.

10. Cecile Hlokofa, interviewed by author, Nov. 5, 2008, Cape Town.
11. Ibid.
12. Mgojo, interview.
13. Ntsebeza, interview.
14. Mmatshilo Motsei, *The Kanga and the Kangaroo Court: Reflections on the Rape Trial of Jacob Zuma* (Johannesburg: Jacana, 2007), 10.
15. Malegapuru William Makgoba ed., *African Renaissance: The New Struggle* (Cape Town: Tafelberg and Mafube, 1999), 153.
16. Mazo Sybil T. MaDlamini Buthelezi, *African Nurse Pioneers in KwaZulu/Natal—1920–2000* (Victoria: Trafford, 2004), 129.
17. Mvuselelo Ngcoya, "*Ubuntu*: Globalization, Accommodation, and Contestation in South Africa" (PhD diss., Faculty of the School of International Service, American University, 2009), 1.
18. Mangosuthu Buthelezi, interviewed by author, Dec. 16, 2009, Ulundi.
19. Finca, interview.
20. Mgojo, interview.
21. Tutu, *No Future Without Forgiveness*, 35.
22. Finca, interview.
23. Bhengu, *Ubuntu*, 50.
24. Bhekithemba Mchunu, interviewed by author, Dec. 13, 2009, Rural area near Ulundi.
25. Stanlake Samkange and Tommie Marie Samkange, *Hunhuism or Ubuntuism: A Zimbabwe Indigenous Political Philosophy* (Salisbury: Graham Publishing, 1980), 38.
26. Ibid.
27. Aninka Claassens, "People and Whites," *The Black Sash* 28, no. 4 (1986): 18.
28. Fred Khumalo, "Drawing Inspiration from the Proud Legacy of Nelson Mandela" (speech delivered to a symposium organized by the Department of Education, Port Elizabeth, Sep. 13, 2008), 1.
29. Buthelezi, interview.
30. Mogobe B. Ramose, *African Philosophy Through Ubuntu* (Harare: Mond Books, 1999), 81.
31. Ifeanyi A. Menkiti, "Persons and Community in African Traditional Thought," in *African Philosophy*, ed. Richard A. Wright (New York: University Press of America, 1984), 172.
32. See Ifeanyi A. Menkiti, "On the Normative Conception of a Person," in *A Companion to African Philosophy*, ed. Kwasi Wiredu (Malden, MA: Blackwell, 2004).
33. See Meyer Fortes, *Religion, Morality and the Person: Essays on Tellensi Religion* (New York: Cambridge University Press, 1987).
34. Kwasi Wiredu, "Introduction: African Philosophy in Our Time," in Wiredu, *A Companion to African Philosophy*, 17.
35. Buthelezi, interview
36. Bhengu, interview
37. Mchunu, interview.
38. In my search for texts on *ubuntu*, Google Books and Google Scholar have been particularly useful as they contain a very large number of texts. Additionally, I have used databases such as JSTOR, Philosophers Index, Web of Science, and Scopus. Future findings may show that my history of how *ubuntu* has been defined in the written sources requires revision, and it is—of course—uncertain to what extent this written history corresponds to the history of how *ubuntu* has been defined orally.
39. See Bhengu, *Ubuntu*, 10.
40. Tom Lodge, *South African Politics since 1994* (Cape Town: David Philip Publishers, 1999), 99.
41. Even though many scholars have suggested that written references to *ubuntu* emerged during the second half of the twentieth century, I have found the following texts from the pre-1950 periods containing the term *ubuntu*: H. H. Hare et al., *I-Testamente entsha yenkosi yetu Ka-Yesu Kristu Gokwamaxosa* (Ishicilelwe Kwisishicilelo Sabra-

Wesli: E-Newton Dale, 1846), Jude 7, 8, 16; John W. Appleyard, *The Kafir Language* (Grahamtown: Wesleyan Missionary Society, 1850), 106; James Perrin, *An English-Kafir Dictionary of the Zulu-Kafir Language: As Spoken by the Tribes of the Colony of Natal* (Pietermaritzburg: May and Davis, 1855), 120; John W. Colenso, *An Elementary Grammar of the Zulu-Kafir Language: Prepared for the Use of Missionaries, and Other Students* (London: Richard Clay, 1855), 7; Lewis Grout, *The Isizulu: A Grammar of the Zulu Language* (Pietermaritzburg: May and Davis, 1859), 398; John W. Colenso, *Inzindatyana zabantu kanye nezindaba zas'eNatal* (Pietermaritzburg: May and Davis, 1859), xli; John W. Colenso, *Zulu-English Dictionary* (Pietermaritzburg: P. Davis, 1861), 354; J. A. Blair et al., *The Collects, Epistles, and Gospels, from the Book of Common Prayer of the Church of England: Translated into Zulu* (Natal: Springvale Mission Station, 1866), 190; Charles Roberts, *The Zulu-Kafir Language Simplified for Beginners* (London: Wesleyan Missionary Society, 1880), 107; American Bible Society, *IBaible eli ingcwele: Eli neTestamente elidala, nelitya, ku kitywa kuzo izilimi zokuqala, ku lotywa ngokwesi-Zulu* (New York: American Bible Society, 1883), 190; Incwadi Yamaculo, *Incwadi yamaculo ndawonye nezikungo nezimiselo zekerike yabazalwana, ebizwayo ngokutiwa yeyama-Moravia* (Herrnhut: Fr. Lindenbein, 1885), 30; Johann G. F. Riedel, *De sluik-en kroesharige rassen tusschen Selebes en Papua* (The Hague: M. Nijhoff, 1886), 236; Lewis Grout, *The Isizulu: A Revised Edition of a Grammar of the Zulu Language; with an Introduction and Appendix* (London: J. F. Shaw, 1893), 290; Charles Roberts, *The Zulu-Kafir Language Simplified for Beginners* (London: K. Paul, Trench, Trübner and Co., 1895), 133; James McLaren, "The Wit and Wisdom of the Bantu as Illustrated in Their Proverbial Sayings," *Suid-Afrikaanse journaal van wetenskap* 14 (1918): 332; Godfrey Callaway, "Further Thoughts about *Ubuntu*," *The East & the West: A Quarterly Review for the Study of Missionary* 23 (1925); S. P. T. Prideaux, "Notes on the Quarterlies," *The Church Missionary Review* 76, no. 849 (1925): 269; Godfrey Callaway, "Manners and Race Relationships," *International Review of Missions* 15, no. 57 (1926): 395; John Kirk, *The Economic Aspects of Native Segregation in South Africa* (London: P. S. King & Son, 1929): 148; A. V. Murray, *The School in the Bush: A Critical Study of the Theory and Practice of Native Education in Africa* (London: Longmans, 1929), xvi; Godfrey Callaway, *The Soul of an African Padre* (London: A. R. Mowbray, 1932), 48; Leonard Barnes, *Zulu Paraclete: A Sentimental Record* (London: P. Davies, 1935), 46; Monica H. Wilson, *Reactions to Conquest: Effects of Contact with Europeans on the Pondo of South Africa* (London: Oxford University Press, 1936), 555; T. L. Davis et al., *Village Education in Africa: Report of the Inter-Territorial 'Jeanes' Conference, Salisbury, S. Rhodesia, May 27th–June 6th, 1935* (Lovedale: Lovedale Press, 1936), 142; Clement M. Doke, "The Earliest Records of Bantu," *Bantu Studies* 12 (1938): 135; Godfrey Callaway et al., *Godfrey Callaway, Missionary in Kaffraria, 1892–1942: His Life and Writings* (London: Society for Promoting Christian Knowledge, 1945), 11, 29, 270; Clement M. Doke, *Text Book of Zulu Grammar* (London: Longmans, Green and Co., 1945), 36, 60; R. H. W. Shepherd and B. G. Paver, *African Contrasts: The Story of a South African People* (Cape Town: Oxford University Press, 1947), 41; Oliver Walker, *Kaffirs are Lively: Being some Backstage Impressions of the South African Democracy* (London: V. Gollancz, 1948), 220.

42. Appleyard, *The Kafir Language*, 106; Perrin, *An English-Kafir Dictionary*, 120; Colenso, *Elementary Grammar*, 7; Colenso, *Zulu-English Dictionary*, 354; Roberts, *Zulu-Kafir Language* [1880], 107; Grout, *Revised Edition of a Grammar*, 290; Roberts, *Zulu-Kafir Language* [1895],133; James McLaren, *A Xhosa Grammar* (Cape Town: Longmans, 1955), 25; Alfred T. Bryant, *Bantu Origins: The People & Their Language* (Cape Town: C. Struik, 1963), 232; Godfrey Callaway, *The Fellowship of the Veld: Sketches of Native Life in South Africa* (New York: Negro University Press, 1969), 22.

43. Callaway, "Manners and Race Relationships," 395; Wilson, *Reactions to Conquest*, 555; Doke, *Text Book*, 60; Walker, *Kaffirs are Lively*, 220; J. Van Sembeek, *A Bemba Grammar* (London: Longmans, Green and Co., 1955), 42; McLaren, *A Xhosa Grammar*, 25; D. M. Malcolm, *A Zulu Manual for Beginners: With Exercises* (Cape Town: Longmans, 1960), 163; Clement M. Doke et al., *The Southern Bantu Languages* (London: Dawsons of Pall Mall, 1967), 54; Firmin Rodegem, *Précis de grammaire rundi* (Brussels:

Story-Scientia, 1967), 129; Callaway, *The Fellowship of the Veld*, 22; Leonard Thompson, *The Oxford History of South Africa: South Africa to 1870*, vol. 1 (New York: Oxford University Press, 1969), 129; A. L. Epstein, "Injury and Liability: Legal Ideas and Implicit Assumptions," *Mankind* 6, no. 9 (1967): 379; B. A. Pauw, *The Second Generation: A Study of the Family among Urbanized Bantu in East London* (Cape Town: Oxford University Press, 1973), 89; Leonard Thompson and Jeffrey Butler, *Change in Contemporary Africa* (Berkeley: University of California Press, 1975), 158, 160; Liz Clarke and Jane Ngobese, *Women without Men: A Study of 150 Families in the Nqutu District of Kwazulu* (Durban: Institute for Black Research, 1975), 34; William S. Livingston, *A Prospect of Liberal Democracy* (Austin: University of Texas Bicentennial Committee, 1979), 128.

44. J. A. Egenbrecht, *Zoeloe-leerboek: Met oefeninge, leesstrukke, wordelys en 'n aantal raaisels en spreekwoorde* (Johannesburg: Voortrekkerpers Beperk, 1962), 22; Egbert De Vries, *Man in Community: Christian Concern for the Human in Changing Society* (New York: Association Press, 1966), 121; Thompson and Butler, *Change in Contemporary Africa*, 158; Stanlake Samkange, *The Mourned One* (London: Heinemann Educational, 1975), 96; Jørgen Lissner, *Namibia 1975: Hope, Fear and Ambiguity* (Geneva: Lutheran World Federation, 1976), 92; Dirk Ziervogel et al., *A Handbook of the Zulu Language* (Pretoria: J. L. van Schaik, 1976), 58; Eileen J. Krige et al., *Social System and Tradition in Southern Africa: Essays in Honour of Eileen Krige* (Cape Town: Oxford University Press, 1978), 152; Jacobus A. Du Plessis, *IsiXhosa* (Parow: Oudiovista, 1978), 48; Steve Biko, *I Write What I Like* (San Francisco: Harper and Row, 1978), 214.

45. John W. Colenso, *An Elementary Grammar of the Zulu-Kafir Language: Prepared for the Use of Missionaries, and Other Students* (London: Richard Clay, 1855), 354; Monica H. Wilson, *Reactions to Conquest: Effects of Contact with Europeans on the Pondo of South Africa* (London: Oxford University Press, 1936), 555; Godfrey Callaway, "Further Thoughts about Ubuntu," *The East & the West: A Quarterly Review for the Study of Missionary* 23 (1925), 22.

46. Colenso, *Zulu-English Dictionary*, 354.

47. Ibid.

48. James McLaren, "The Wit and Wisdom of the Bantu as Illustrated in Their Proverbial Sayings," *Suid-Afrikaanse journaal van wetenskap* 14 (1918), 332.

49. S. P. T. Prideaux, "Notes on the Quarterlies," *The Church Missionary Review* 76, no. 849 (1925): 269; Absolom Vilakazi, *Zulu Transformations: A Study of the Dynamics of Social Change* (Pietermaritzburg: University of Natal Press, 1962), 60; C. L. S. Nyembezi, *Zulu Proverbs* (Johannesburg: Witwatersrand University Press, 1963), 47; C. L. S. Nyembezi, *Learn More Zulu* (Pietermaritzburg: Shuter and Schooter, 1970), 16.

50. Leonard Barnes, *Zulu Paraclete: A Sentimental Record* (London: P. Davies, 1935), 46.

51. Callaway et al., *Godfrey Callaway*, 11.

52. Ibid.

53. Ibid., 29.

54. Shepherd and Paver, *African Contrasts*, 41.

55. Edgar H. Brookes, *R. J.: In Appreciation of the Life of John David Rheinallt Jones and His Work for the Betterment of Race Relations in Southern Africa* (Johannesburg: Transvaal Printing and Photo-Lithographers, 1953), 20.

56. Van Sembeek, *A Bemba Grammar*, 42; Callaway, *The Fellowship of the Veld*, 22.

57. Alexis Kagame, *La Philosophie Bantu-rwandaise de l'être* (Brussels: Académie royale des sciences coloniales, 1955), 53.

58. Margaret Read, *Children of their Fathers: Growing up among the Ngoni of Nyasaland* (London: Methuen, 1959), 149; Margaret Read, *Children of their Fathers: Growing up among the Ngoni of Malawi* (New York: Holt, Rinehart and Winston, 1968), 80.

59. Noni Jabavu, *Drawn in Colour: African Contrasts* (London: Murray, 1960), 4.

60. Nyembezi, *Zulu Proverbs*, 47.

61. Ibid.

62. D. H. Reader, *Zulu Tribe in Transition: The Makhanya of Southern Natal* (Manchester: Manchester University Press, 1966), 175.

63. Rodegem, *Précis de grammaire rundi*, 129.
64. Ibid.; Callaway, *The Fellowship of the Veld*, 22.
65. Sabra Study Group of Fort Hare, *The Ciskey—A Bantu Homeland: A General Survey* (Fort Hare: Fort Hare University Press, 1971), 121.
66. South African Department of Bantu Education, *Xhosa: Terminologie en spelreëls* (Pretoria: Staatsdrukker, 1972), 129.
67. South African Department of Bantu Education, *Zoeloe terminologie en spelreëls* (Pretoria: Staatsdrukker, 1972), 153.
68. A. C. Jordan, *Tales from Southern Africa* (Berkeley: University of California Press, 1973), 228.
69. B. A. Pauw, *Christianity and Xhosa Tradition: Belief and Ritual among Xhosa-Speaking Christians* (Cape Town: Oxford University Press, 1975), 117.
70. Thompson and Butler, *Change in Contemporary Africa*, 213.
71. Clarke and Ngobese, *Women without Men*, 61.
72. Penelope Hetherington, *British Paternalism and Africa, 1920–1940* (London: F. Cass, 1978), 68.
73. Alexandre Kimenyi, *Studies in Kinyarwanda and Bantu Phonology* (Edmonton: Linguistic Research, 1979), 75.
74. See for instance: Murray, *The School in the Bush*, 105; Davis et al., *Village Education in Africa*, 142; Doke, *Text Book*, 36; Edwin William Smith, *The Blessed Missionaries* (Cape Town: Oxford University Press, 1950), 18; Southern Rhodesian Department of Native Affairs, *NADA: The Southern Rhodesia Native Affairs Department Annual* (Salisbury: Southern Rhodesian Department of Native Affairs, 1950), 34; G. H. Calpin et al., *The South African Way of Life: Values and Ideals of a Multi-Racial Society* (New York: Columbia University Press, 1953), 56; Brookes, *John David Rheinallt Jones*, 20; Van Sembeek, *A Bemba Grammar*, 42; C. P. Groves, *The Planting of Christianity in Africa* (London: Lutterworth Press, 1958), 20; Jabavu, *Drawn in Colour*, 4; Callaway, *The Fellowship of the Veld*, 22; Lissner, *Namibia 1975*, 92; Krige et al., *Social System and Tradition*, 152.
75. Doke, *Text Book*, 36; Calpin et al., *The South African Way of Life*, 56.
76. Davis et al., *Village Education in Africa*, 142.
77. Smith, *The Blessed Missionaries*, 18.
78. Southern Rhodesian Department of Native Affairs, *NADA*, 34.
79. Jabavu, *Drawn in Colour*, 4; Thompson and Butler, *Change in Contemporary Africa*, 158.
80. Pauw, *The Second Generation*, 89.
81. Alan Paton, *Ah, but Your Land is Beautiful* (New York: Scribner, 1983), 62.
82. J. Suggit and M. Goedhals, *Change and Challenge: Essays Commemorating the 150th Anniversary of Robert Gray as First Bishop of Cape Town* (Marshalltown: Church of the Province of Southern Africa, 1998), 112.
83. Emmanuel M. Kolini and Peter R. Holmes, *Rethinking Life: What the Church Can Learn from Africa* (Colorado Springs: Authentic Publishing, 2010), 70.
84. Jordan Kush Ngubane, *An African Explains Apartheid* (London: Pall Mall Press, 1963), 76.
85. Jordan Kush Ngubane, *Conflicts of Minds* (New York: Books in Focus, 1979), 113.
86. Newell Snow Booth, *African Religions: A Symposium* (New York: NOK Publishers, 1977), 15.
87. Philip Mayer, *Black Villagers in an Industrial Society: Anthropological Perspectives on Labour Migration in South Africa* (Cape Town: Oxford University Press, 1980), 70.
88. Ramose, *African Philosophy through Ubuntu*, 64.
89. James R. Cochrane, "Salvation and the Reconstruction of Society," in *Happiness, Well-being and the Meaning of Life: A Dialogue of Social Science and Religion*, ed. Vincent Brümer and Marcel Sarot (Kampen: Kok Pharos Publishing House, 1996), 87.
90. Elza Venter, "The Notion of *Ubuntu* and Communalism in African Educational Discourse," *Studies in Philosophy and Education* 23, no. 2–3 (2004): 149.
91. Motsei, *The Kanga and the Kangaroo Court*, 10.

92. Cornel W. du Toit, *The Integrity of the Human Person in an African Context: Perspectives from Science and Religion* (Pretoria: Research Institute for Theology and Religion University of South Africa, 2004), 33.
93. Megan Shore, *Religion and Conflict Resolution: Christianity and South Africa's Truth and Reconciliation Commission* (Farnham: Ashgate, 2009), 135.
94. Africa Institute of South Africa, *Communications of the Africa Institute* (Pretoria: Africa Institute of South Africa, 1975), 177; W. J. Breytenbach, *Tuislande: selfregering en politieke partye* (Pretoria: Africa Institute of South Africa, 1975), 177; Ngubane, *Conflicts of Minds*, 261.
95. Peter L. Berger and Bobby Godsell, ed., *A Future South Africa: Visions, Strategies, and Realities* (Cape Town: Human & Rousseau, 1988), 176.
96. Erasmus D. Prinsloo, "*Ubuntu* Culture and Participatory Management," in *The African Philosophy Reader*, ed. Peter Hendrik Coetzee and A. P. J. Roux (London: Routledge, 1998), 42.
97. Patrick Lenta, "The Changing Face of the Law: *Ubuntu*, Religion and the Politics of Postcolonial Legality," in *Explorations in Contemporary Continental Philosophy of Religion*, ed. Deane-Peter Baker and Patrick Maxwell (Amsterdam: Editions Rodopi B. V., 2003), 156.
98. Tutu, *No Future Without Forgiveness*, 34.
99. Charmaine McEachern, *Narratives of Nation Media, Memory and Representation in the Making of the New South Africa* (New York: Nova Science Publishers, 2002), 31.
100. Amy E. Ansell, "Two Nations of Discourse: Mapping Racial Ideologies in Post-Apartheid South Africa," in *The New Black: Alternative Paradigms and Strategies for the 21st Century*, ed. Rodney D. Coates and Rutledge M. Dennis (Oxford: Elsevier, 2007), 318.
101. Sindre Bangstad, *Global Flows, Local Appropriations: Facets of Secularisation and Re-Islamization among Contemporary Cape Muslims* (Leiden: Amsterdam University Press, 2007), 49.
102. Dalene M. Swanson, "Values in Shadows: A Critical Contribution to Values Education in Our Time," in *International Research Handbook on Values, Education and Student Wellbeing*, ed. Terry Lovat, Ron Toomey and Neville Clement (Dordrecht: Springer, 2010), 47.
103. Geoffrey K. Ronaldson, "Diversity in the Rainbow Nation of South Africa," in *Analysis of Social Interaction Systems: SYMLOG Research and Applications*, ed. A. Paul Hare et al. (Lanham, MD: University Press of America, 2005), 153.
104. Mark Albion, *More Than Money: Questions Every MBA Needs to Answer* (San Francisco: Berrett-Koehler Publishers, 2008), 85.

SEVEN
Ubuntu, History, and Politics

The call for a return to *ubuntu*, first discussed in chapter two, is based on the idea that *ubuntu* was important in the past. But does this idea correspond to historical fact, and is such a correspondence even important? Could the post-apartheid claim about *ubuntu's* ancient roots represent a kind of history in which the aim is not to present history as it really was, but rather to create specific futures?

As a background for discussing such questions, I want to present some rather thought-provoking ideas from Nietzsche's essay "History in the Service and Disservice of Life."[1] In this essay, Nietzsche states: "Only insofar as history serves life do we wish to serve history."[2] We need history for life and action, he explains, and then he presents a hope for the future: "If only we could get better at studying history in pursuit of life!"[3] The essay is a harsh attack on historicism, which he describes as our time's dominant historical orientation.[4] The problem is that historicism is obsessed with how the past really was. "[W]e are all suffering from the ravages of historical fever"[5] is Nietzsche's interesting and provocative claim.

Nietzsche emphasizes that the past can be a burden: an insight shared by many who have been the victims of human rights violations (cf. chapter three). For the man who cannot forget, the past is—Nietzsche tells us—a chain, which runs with him however far or fast he runs. The past becomes a heavy, often invisible load that will continue to grow and to obstruct his movement.[6] For Nietzsche, this implies that happiness requires the ability to forget: "The man who cannot pause upon the threshold of the moment, forgetting the entire past, the man who cannot pivot on a tiny point like a goddess of victory, without dizziness or fear, will never know happiness."[7]

In Nietzsche's view, happiness requires us to forget the burdens of the past, and that we stop being so obsessed with the truth about the past. Rather, the past should be used, constructed, and invented in ways that help man to live a happy and healthy life in the present. Thus Nietzsche admires "the man of action" (a phrase from Goethe), who uses the past for the purposes of the present and in doing so is unscrupulous and forgetful: "He forgets almost everything in order to accomplish just one thing; he is unjust to what lies behind him, and he knows only one truth: what must be done now."[8] The man of action does not thoroughly understand the past, and this is good, for if he did, the past would lose its flexibility and usefulness. As Nietzsche writes, "A historical phenomenon which is clearly and thoroughly understood, and which is resolved into a phenomenon of knowledge, is dead to the person who has understood it."[9]

ANTIQUARIAN HISTORY

Nietzsche claims that antiquarian history is a kind of history that serves life. He explains that the man who makes antiquarian history preserves and venerates the past, and looks back with love and loyalty to his origin.[10] An important quality of such a man is that he has an ability to create a clear picture of what the past was like, even though the past is concealed beneath dark and confusing centuries: "At times he even greets the spirit of his people across the vast distance of dark and confusing centuries as though it were his own."[11] The man who makes antiquarian history has gifts of "empathy and a feeling for the future, a nose for almost obliterated traces, an instinctive capacity for reading accurately a past still concealed beneath many later layers."[12]

Nietzsche believes that antiquarian history is particularly relevant to historically less-favored people because it fills their condition with a feeling of pleasure and contentment. As religion is a kind of "opium," satisfying and pacifying people in Marx's thinking,[13] so is antiquarian history a kind of "opium" in Nietzsche's account; but unlike Marx, Nietzsche believes that the opium effect is positive:

> How could history better serve life than by binding less-favored races and populations to their native land and native customs, by settling them in one place, and preventing them from straying beyond their borders in search of better land, and competing for that in war? At times it seems as though stubbornness and unreason are the ties that bind the individual to these companions and environments, these tedious customs, these barren mountain ridges. But this is the healthiest, most generally beneficial sort of unreason.[14]

Antiquarian history provides man with a clear and healthy sense of rootedness. In fact, the man who makes antiquarian history can, according to

Nietzsche, be compared metaphorically to a tree standing above ground and having a clear idea of what its own root ball looks like from simply looking at its own visible branches. He observes:

> Now, clearly this [antiquarian history] is not the condition likeliest to enable a man to reduce the past to pure knowledge. So in this case too we observe [. . .] that the past itself suffers so long as history serves life and is governed by the instinct of life.[15]

THE AFRICAN RENAISSANCE AND *UBUNTU*

Thabo Mbeki was deputy president under Mandela and later himself president from 1999 to 2008. Mbeki has, in my opinion, been a man of action in Nietzsche's sense: a producer of antiquarian history in connection with his call for an African renaissance. Among the political leaders of post-apartheid South Africa, Mbeki is the one who has most actively used references to the African precolonial past, and specifically references to *ubuntu*, in his political project.

It was Mbeki who popularized the notion of an "African renaissance," though he did not coin this expression. The oldest text in which I have found the expression is Edwin William Smith's *The Way of White Fields in Rhodesia: A Survey of Christian Enterprise in Northern and Southern Rhodesia*, dating from 1928. In this book, a section entitled "The Era of African Renaissance" consists primarily of a long quote from an address by the Reverend John White to the Southern Rhodesia Missionary Conference in August 1926. Part of this passage reads:

> Since I set foot in Africa over thirty years ago a profound change has taken place in the entire outlook of the native people of this sub-continent. Through the public press and by various other authorities we are being constantly reminded of what is called the dawning of Bantu race-consciousness; of his restlessness, under white domination; of his dissatisfaction with his social, industrial and political status. To those who look below the surface of things are the symptoms of a profound psychological revolution that is silently, slowly but surely, going on. In short we are witnessing a nation in its birth-throes.[16]

In his speech to the United Nations University on April 9, 1998, entitled "The African Renaissance, South Africa and the World," Mbeki said: "I would dare say that confidence [among Africans], in part, derives from a rediscovery of ourselves, from the fact that, perforce, as one would who is critical of oneself, we had to undertake a voyage of discovery into our antecedents, our own past, as Africans." In "The African Renaissance Statement," given on August 13, 1998, he also explained: "To perpetuate their imperial domination over the peoples of Africa, the colonizers sought to enslave the African mind and to destroy the African soul." Consequently "The beginning of our rebirth as a Continent must be our own rediscovery of our soul."[17] In this Mbeki echoed the views of earlier African leaders, including Nyerere, who, as we saw in chapter two, wrote: "Any dominating group seeks to destroy the confidence of those they dominate because this helps them to maintain their position."[18] Mbeki was also not the first South African leader to call for Africanization and a rediscovery of the African soul. During apartheid, this call was for example made by Steve Biko, the leader of Black Consciousness, who explained: "Since that unfortunate date—1652—we have experienced a process of acculturation."[19] Biko wrote that "part of the approach envisaged in bringing about 'black consciousness' has to be directed to the past, to seek to rewrite the history of the black man and to produce in it the heroes who form the core of the African Background."[20] It is, he noted, "through the evolution of our genuine culture that our identity can be fully rediscovered."[21]

Mbeki emphasized that it was the Africans themselves who must bring about the African renaissance, and that they were capable of so doing because they had done great things before:

> in the end, an entire epoch in human history, the epoch of colonialism and white foreign rule, progressed to its ultimate historical burial grounds because [. . .] the Africans dared to stand up to say the new must be born, whatever the sacrifice we have to make—Africa must be free!"[22]

In the same speech, Mbeki said: "The simple phrase 'We are our own liberators!' is the epitaph on the gravestone of every African who dared to carry the vision in his or her heart of African reborn." He added:

> Unless we are able to answer the question "Who were we?" we will not be able to answer the question "What shall we be?" This complex exercise [of the African renaissance], which can be stated in simple terms, links the past to the future and speaks to the interconnection between an empowering process of restoration and the consequences or the response to the acquisition of that newly restored power to create something new.

THE POLITICAL USE OF *UBUNTU*

Mbeki has made active use of *ubuntu* in his African renaissance project. On the eve of the 1999 election that made him president, he held a meeting with Augustine Shutte, a South African moral philosopher and *ubuntu* scholar. Shutte explains that during his meeting with Mbeki:

> He [Mbeki] spoke to us of a "moral vacuum" in South Africa that had the potential to make the country ungovernable. Crime and corruption were just the outward signs of a sickness of the soul that was a legacy of apartheid. The separateness and conflict inevitable in a multicultural society such as South Africa had been intensified by apartheid. It was

however the struggle against apartheid that had brought different groups together on the basis of shared values. Now that had gone and, in spite of a fine constitution and democratic elections, South Africa is threatened with disintegration. People have lost touch with the common humanity we share. A spirit of self-interest is growing. What South Africa needs more than anything is an RDP [Reconstruction and Development Program] of the spirit. Mr Mbeki asked us for help in dealing with this state of affairs.[23]

After his meeting with Mbeki, Shutte initiated a project to explore *ubuntu's* moral potential in post-apartheid South Africa. With the support of Mbeki's government, this project led to the publication of Shutte's book, *Ubuntu: An Ethic for a New South Africa* (2001). Shutte has told me that:

The book itself was a result of the Ubuntu Project which I initiated with Mbeki's blessing after my meeting with him in Pretoria on the eve of the 1999 elections that made him president. Two members of the group I formed were appointed by him, Melanie Verwoerd and Ebrahim Rasool. It was a very high-powered group indeed and did a lot to help me with the book.[24]

During his presidency, Mbeki continuously promoted the idea that *ubuntu* should be an ethic for the new South Africa. He emphasized that the spirit of *ubuntu* is something "which we should strive to implant in the very bosom of the new South Africa that is being born—[*ubuntu* is] the food of the soul that would inspire all our people to say that they are proud to be South African!"[25] Furthermore, in 2005, Mbeki suggested the founding of a task force with the purpose of exploring how to make better use of *ubuntu* in nation building:

Clearly, we have a responsibility to utilize the many positive attributes of *ubuntu* to build a non-racial, non-sexist and united South Africa. We also have to use to better effect the value and ethos of *ubuntu* in our Moral Regeneration Campaign. This we should do because I am confident that all South Africans, black and white, will agree that this value system [of *ubuntu*] should characterize a South African.[26]

In 2006, one year after the statement reproduced above, *ubuntu* became actively incorporated into the agenda of South Africa's National Heritage Council (NHC). In a summary of its activities in 2006, the NHC explains that:

In partnership with the African Renaissance Centre of UNISA [University of South Africa], the NHC hosted the National Question and National Identity Conference. The delegates debated issues around defining the national identity of South Africans in the context of a diverse multi-cultural society that at the same time has a shared history. The [first annual] National Ubuntu Imbizo was launched in Botshabelo, Mpumalanga from 16 to 17 November 2006 as a dedicated campaign to revive the values of *ubuntu*. Over 2,000 people attended. President Nelson Mandela was awarded the first Ubuntu Award.[27]

Two years later, in 2008, the NHC's campaign "Ubuntu in Nation Building" was symbolically launched at the Walter Sisulu Freedom Square, the site at which the Freedom Charter had been adopted at the Congress of the People in 1955. NHC explains:

> The *ubuntu* campaign recognizes and encourages every citizen to embrace the positive values of humanity as one of the intangible cultural heritages of the African people. The campaign promotes love—honesty—compassion—forgiveness—humility and unity. The citizens of South Africa participate in the campaign by nominating their own community members who live these values. Information about the work of these nominated Ubuntu Champions is shared with the entire population to appreciate and possibly emulate—thereby contributing to social cohesion and nation building.[28]

It is evident that there has been a government-led project to infuse South African identity with *ubuntu*, and Mbeki has been the man carrying the project's banner. He has emphasized that a *return* to *ubuntu* (see chapter two) is essential because:

> many of our communities have abandoned the central tenets of our value system of *ubuntu* which for centuries ensured that our people acted responsible and respectfully toward one another, giving due regard to the objective to respect the dignity of every individual regardless of their status in society, concerned to protect the most vulnerable among us.[29]

For Mbeki, it is beyond question that "[t]he spirit of *ubuntu* which enshrined the values of group solidarity, compassion, respect, human dignity and collective unity characterized the lifestyles of our forebears."[30] As the "man of action" in Nietzsche's account, he has a distinctive ability to see clearly what the past was like and states, for example, that the Africans who were the first to encounter Europeans were imbued with *ubuntu*:

> As we know, or should know, when Bartholomew Dias and later Vasco da Gama sailed past the Cape to the East, the first people they encountered in this part of Africa were the Khoi and the San. Although initially suspicious of the stranger that had docked on their shores, these Africans, imbued with the spirit of *ubuntu*, welcomed those Europeans and gave them the best African hospitality that still characterizes our people today. Jan van Riebeeck and his Dutch companions were received with the same hospitality when they arrived in 1652.[31]

Clearly, Mbeki is not a historical scholar, but a politician with a nose for the usefulness of history. I believe he is a man of action in Nietzsche's sense, making antiquarian history by preserving and venerating the past in order to establish a specific African moral identity. In doing so, he demonstrates an ability to create a clear picture of what the African past was like even though the past—to use Nietzsche's words—is concealed beneath dark and confusing centuries.

Ubuntu has evidently been a political instrument for Mbeki, something that he could use to correct and morally educate his fellow South Africans. For example, Mbeki referred to *ubuntu* to challenge the growing individualism in society when he said: "our society has been captured by a rapacious individualism which is corroding our social cohesion, which is repudiating the value and practice of human solidarity, and which totally rejects the fundamental precept of *ubuntu—umntu ngumntu ngabanye*!"[32] Furthermore, when South Africans committed xenophobic violence against immigrants in 2008, Mbeki said:

> We the offspring and heirs to the noble spirit and vision of African unity and solidarity advanced by our giants of thought and action, Tiyo Soga, J. G. Xaba, and Pixley Seme, have gathered here today with heads bowed in shame, because some in our communities acted in ways that communicated the message that the values of *ubuntu* are dead, and that they lie entombed in the graves of the cadavers of people who died ostensibly solely because they came among us as travelers in search of refuge. . . . We must pledge that never again will we allow anybody bring shame to our nation by betraying the values of *ubuntu* and committing crimes against our visitors and travelers, thus to besmirch the character of the eminently good human beings who constitute our nation as people afflicted by the cancerous disease of xenophobia.[33]

According to Mbeki, *ubuntu* has been central to the politics of the post-apartheid ANC government. This conviction is reflected in, for example, the speech he gave on being forced to step down as president in 2008 because of internal disputes in the ANC:

> Indeed the work we have done in pursuit of the vision and principles of our liberation has at all times been based on the age-old values of *ubuntu*, of selflessness, sacrifice and service in a manner that ensures that the interest of the people take precedence over our desire as individuals. I truly believe that the governments in which I have been privileged to serve have acted and worked in the true spirit of these important values. Based on the values of *ubuntu*, the significance of which we learned at the feet of such giants of our struggle as Chief Albert Luthuli, O. R. Tambo, Nelson Mandela and others, we as government embarked, from 1994, on policies and programs directed at pulling the people of South Africa out of the morass of poverty and ensuring that we build a stable, developing and prosperous country.[34]

RAMOSE VERSUS VAN BINSBERGEN

The debate between Ramose and Van Binsbergen on *ubuntu* turns on the question whether *ubuntu* was the value-orientation of precolonial Southern African villages—which is the position reflected in Mbeki's speeches—or rather a contemporary academic and political construct. The first position is found in Ramose's book *African Philosophy Through Ubuntu*, while the second is advocated by Van Binsbergen in his article "*Ubuntu* and the Globalization of Southern African Thought and Society."[35]

As highlighted by Van Binsbergen, "Ramose sees in *ubuntu* the value-orientation of precolonial Southern African villages, which in his opinion is faithfully rendered in contemporary academic statements of *ubuntu* philosophy."[36] Furthermore, Ramose believes that a revival of *ubuntu* could be an antidote for the threatening forces of globalization that are transmitting rather contagious negative Western ideas and ways of life in Africa. Van Binsbergen, on the other hand, has a fundamentally different interpretation of the relationship between globalization and *ubuntu*: "For Ramose, globalization is an outside phenomenon to be countered by *ubuntu*; I on the contrary argue that both contemporary Southern Africa, and *ubuntu* itself, are among the products of globalization, and can only be understood as such products."[37] Additionally, Van Binsbergen explains that "although *ubuntu* philosophy may be able to curb some (certainly not all) of the contemporary traumatic effects of globalization/conquest, it is a new thing in a globalized format, not a perennial village thing in an authentic format."[38]

Another thought-provoking claim by Van Binsbergen is that the majority of the population in Southern Africa do not know or live *ubuntu* by virtue of any continuity with village life: "They have to be educated to pursue (under the name of *ubuntu*) a *global and urban reformulation* of village values [italic in original]."[39] He continues: "And they learn this on the authority, not of traditional diviner-priests to whom one cannot appeal in the globalized space without great personal embarrassment, but of recognized opinion leaders of the globalized center: politicians, university intellectuals."[40] In other words, it is politicians like Mbeki and university intellectuals like Shutte who educate Africans about *ubuntu*.

Van Binsbergen is also convinced that the *ubuntu* statements by contemporary opinion leaders are inherently ideological and represent dreams of the past and the periphery:

> Such dreams about the past and the periphery are articulated, not because the speaker proposes to retire there personally or wishes to exhort other people to take up effective residence there, but because of the inspiring modeling power with regard to central national and even global issues—in other words because of these dreams' alleged persua-

sive/perlocutionary nature outside the peripheral domain in which they are claimed to originate and to which they refer back.[41]

Thus, drawing on Austin's book *How to do Things with Words*, Van Binsbergen points to the ideological nature of contemporary *ubuntu* statements. He highlights that such statements represent perlocutionary (in other words, persuasive) rather than locutionary (or factual) speech acts.

In my view, Ramose's and Van Binsbergen's positions on *ubuntu* represent a Scylla and a Charybdis. I wish to argue for a middle course that manages to steer between the two, and I showed in chapter six that the word *ubuntu* is found in texts more than 150 years old, and that the contemporary interpretation of *ubuntu* as a moral quality is present in the early texts. A significant weakness with Van Binsbergen's position is that he does not recognize that some contemporary interpretations of *ubuntu* have a long history. He writes, in fact, as already demonstrated, that according to his knowledge the oldest publication on *ubuntu* is the Samkanges' *Hunhunism or Ubuntuism,* published in 1980.[42]

The problem with Ramose's position, on the other hand, is that it reduces *ubuntu* to something historical and does not recognize *ubuntu's* instrumentalist dimensions. These dimensions are clearly recognized by Van Binsbergen, who emphasizes that *ubuntu* is used as a political tool. In this connection I completely agree with Van Binsbergen that some statements about *ubuntu* have a perlocutionary nature. For example, Mbeki's antiquarian *ubuntu* history is inherently perlocutionary: it is first and foremost about persuading South Africans to buy into the *ubuntu* ideology that he presents. The stories he tells of *ubuntu's* roles in the past contribute to the persuasion, and this is—in my interpretation—their primary function. Whether these stories are factual or not is of less importance.

Clearly, there is a dimension of power to the *ubuntu* talk in post-apartheid South Africa. Marx and Engels emphasize that there is a clear link between ideas and power, since in every epoch the ideas of the rulers are the ruling ideas.[43] Under apartheid, the ruling ideas in society were about segregation, while in post-apartheid South Africa, *ubuntu* ideas of interconnectedness, often expressed referring to the proverb *umuntu ngumuntu ngabantu,* came to rule and were developed into a political ideology of the ANC government. Furthermore, just as segregation ideas served to legitimize the segregation politics of the apartheid government, so have *ubuntu* ideas of interconnectedness served to legitimize the reconciliation politics after apartheid. In this connection I recall Wilson's reasonable words: that *ubuntu* became "the Africanist wrapping used to sell a reconciliatory version of human rights talk to black South Africans."[44]

The findings that I have presented in this book emphasizes that *ubuntu* is an ideological concept with multiple meanings, some of which have been employed in the context of transitional justice in post-apartheid South Africa. In this context, it is noteworthy, however, that most of the claims about a close connection between the TRC and *ubuntu* were made after the TRC process. Thus they represent *retrospective* interpretations. I find it likely that some of these retrospective interpretations were inspired by the increasing hype around *ubuntu* during the presidency of Mbeki. The Mbeki government highlighted the importance of *ubuntu* in post-apartheid South Africa, and this could be part of the reason why so many began to claim that *ubuntu* had been a significant element in the TRC process. However, the word *ubuntu* was used only very intermittently in the TRC hearings; and TRC commissioners and committee members have told me that they did not discuss *ubuntu*, and that *ubuntu* was never a policy of the TRC.

NOTES

1. Friedrich Nietzsche, "History in the Service and Disservice of Life," in *Unmodern Observations*, ed. William Arrowsmith (New Haven, CT: Yale University Press, 1990).
2. Ibid., 87.
3. Ibid., 94.
4. Ibid., 87.
5. Ibid., 88.
6. Ibid., 89.
7. Ibid.
8. Ibid., 92.
9. Ibid., 94.
10. Ibid., 100.
11. Ibid.
12. Ibid.
13. Marx writes that "Religion is the sigh of the oppressed creature, the heart of a heartless world and the soul of soulless conditions. It is the opium of the people." Karl Marx, *Critique of Hegel's "Philosophy of Right,"* ed. Joseph O'Malley (Cambridge: Cambridge University Press, 1982), 131.
14. Nietzsche, "History in the Service and Disservice of Life," 100.
15. Ibid., 101.
16. Edwin William Smith, *The Way of the White Fields in Rhodesia: A Survey of Christian Enterprise in Northern and Southern Rhodesia* (London: World Dominion Press, 1928), 142.
17. Thabo Mbeki. "The African Renaissance Statement." Gallagher Estate, Aug. 13, 1998.
18. Nyerere, *Freedom and Unity*, 3.
19. Steve Biko, *I Write What I Like* (San Francisco: Harper and Row, 1978), 40.
20. Ibid., 29.
21. Ibid., 71.
22. Thabo Mbeki, "The African Renaissance, South Africa and the World" (speech, United Nations University, Apr. 9, 1998).
23. Augustine Shutte, "The Common Good Project" (unpublished concept paper, 2000, received in an e-mail from Shutte, Dec. 13, 2010).
24. Augustine Shutte, e-mail to author, Nov. 21, 2010.
25. Thabo Mbeki, "Nelson Mandela Memorial Lecture" (lecture, University of Witwatersrand, July 29, 2006).

26. Thabo Mbeki, "Address at the Heritage Day Celebrations" (speech, Taung, North West Province, Sep. 24, 2005).

27. National Heritage Council, "Building a Nation: Proud of its African Heritage," 2014 brochure, accessed Nov. 21, 2016, http://www.nhc.org.za/wp-content/uploads/2014/03/NHC-Heritage-brochure-A4-Pages.pdf.

28. National Heritage Council, "Ubuntu," Projects on the Website of the National Heritage Council, accessed Nov. 21, 2016, http://www.nhc.org.za/project/ubuntu/.

29. Thabo Mbeki, "Address at the Opening of the National House of Traditional Leaders" (speech, City of Tshwane, May 4, 2006).

30. Thabo Mbeki, "Address on the Occasion of Heritage Day" (speech, Cape Town, Sep. 24, 2006).

31. Mbeki, "Address on the Occasion of Heritage Day," 2006.

32. Thabo Mbeki, "Steve Biko Memorial Lecture" (lecture delivered on the occasion of the 30th anniversary of the death of Stephen Bantu Biko, Cape Town, Sep. 12, 2007).

33. Thabo Mbeki, "National Tribute in Remembrance of Xenophobic Attacks Victims" (speech, Tshwane, July 3, 2008).

34. Mbeki, "Resignation Speech."

35. See also J. A. Bewaji and Mogobe B. Ramose, "The Bewaji, Van Binsbergen and Ramose Debate on *Ubuntu*," *South African Journal of Philosophy* 22, no. 4 (2003). The main positions in the debate are those of Ramose and Van Binsbergen, while Bewaji is "merely" a supporter of Ramose (though he has a few critical remarks to Ramose's book).

36. Wim van Binsbergen, "*Ubuntu* and the Globalization of Southern African Thought and Society," Quest 15, no. 1–2 (2001): 62.

37. Ibid.

38. Ibid.

39. Ibid., 64.

40. Ibid.

41. Ibid., 60.

42. Ibid., 82.

43. Karl Marx and Frederick Engels, *The German Ideology*, ed. C. J. Arthur (New York: International Publishers, 1970), 64.

44. Richard A. Wilson, *The Politics of Truth and Reconciliation in South Africa: Legitimizing the Post-Apartheid State* (Cambridge: Cambridge University Press, 2001), 13.

EIGHT
Postscript

As demonstrated in the foregoing chapters, this book presents a collective discourse on African philosophy which—unlike ethnophilosophy—takes differences, historical developments, and social contexts seriously.

I hope that my use of qualitative interviews and historical text investigations will inspire other scholars of African philosophy to use similar methods to investigate the ideas of Africans, whether the ideas of Africans in general or the ideas found within specific groups. By means of thorough empirical investigations, we will gain a much more nuanced understanding of such ideas, and we will avoid committing the ethnophilosophical fallacy of producing myths about groups possessing a set of shared, static ideas.

After conducting empirical investigations by means of interviews and text investigations, a second step of this "Gade discourse" on African philosophy is to reflect on the empirical findings. I have done that in this book by suggesting that the *ubuntu* talk in post-apartheid South Africa has to be understood within the broader context of narratives of return in postcolonial Africa, and that the ideas about a return to *ubuntu* are political in nature and represent an antiquarian kind of history.

My discourse on African philosophy should not be limited to the topic of *ubuntu*. In fact, scholars of African philosophy could use it to explore all the other topics that have been dealt with by ethnophilosophers. In his book *Bantu Philosophy*, Tempels looks into diverse topics within ontology, epistemology, ethics and law. Perhaps some of Tempels's sweeping ethnophilosophical generalizations within these areas could be revised by means of interviews and historical text investigations. That is a task worth undertaking by scholars of African philosophy.

Bibliography

Africa Institute of South Africa. *Communications of the Africa Institute*. Pretoria: Africa Institute of South Africa, 1975.
Albion, Mark. *More Than Money: Questions Every MBA Needs to Answer*. San Francisco: Berrett-Koehler Publishers, 2008.
American Bible Society, *IBaible eli ingcwele: Eli neTestamente elidala, nelitya, ku kitywa kuzo izilimi zokuqala, ku lotywa ngokwesi-Zulu*. New York: American Bible Society, 1883.
Ansell, Amy E. "Two Nations of Discourse: Mapping Racial Ideologies in Post-Apartheid South Africa." In *The New Black: Alternative Paradigms and Strategies for the 21st Century*, edited by Rodney D. Coates and Rutledge M. Dennis. Oxford: Elsevier, 2007.
Appleyard, John W. *The Kafir Language*. Grahamtown: Wesleyan Missionary Society, 1850.
Arendt, Hannah. *On Violence*. San Diego: Harvest Book, 1970.
Austin, John L. *How to Do Things with Words*. Oxford: Oxford University Press, 1962.
Azanian Peoples Organization and Others v. The President of South Africa and Others, *No. CCT 17/96*. Constitutional Court of South Africa, July 25, 1ho996. http://www.justice.gov.za/trc/legal/azapo.htm.
Bangstad, Sindre. *Global Flows, Local Appropriations: Facets of Secularisation and Re-Islamization among Contemporary Cape Muslims*. Leiden: Amsterdam University Press, 2007.
Barnes, Leonard. *Zulu Paraclete: A Sentimental Record*. London: P. Davies, 1935.
Bell, Richard. *Rethinking Justice: Restoring Our Humanity*. Lanham, MD: Lexington Books, 2007.
———. *Understanding African Philosophy: A Cross-Cultural Approach to Classical and Contemporary Issues*. New York: Routledge, 2002.
Berger, Peter L., and Bobby Godsell, ed. *A Future South Africa: Visions, Strategies, and Realities*. Cape Town: Human & Rousseau, 1988.
Bewaji, J. A. and Mogobe B. Ramose. "The Bewaji, Van Binsbergen and Ramose Debate on *Ubuntu*." *South African Journal of Philosophy* 22, no. 4 (2003): 378–415.
Bhengu, Mfuniselwa J. *Ubuntu: The Essence of Democracy*. Cape Town: Novalis Press, 1996.
Biko, Steve. *I Write What I Like*. San Francisco: Harper and Row, 1978.
Blair, J. A. et al. *The Collects, Epistles, and Gospels, from the Book of Common Prayer of the Church of England—Translated into Zulu*. Natal: Springvale Mission Station, 1866.
Booth, Newell Snow. *African Religions: A Symposium*. New York: NOK Publishers, 1977.
Boraine, Alex. *A Country Unmasked: Inside South Africa's Truth and Reconciliation Commission*. Oxford: Oxford University Press, 2000.
Breytenbach, W. J. *Tuislande: selfregering en politieke partye*. Pretoria: Africa Institute of South Africa, 1975.
Brookes, Edgar H. *R. J.: In Appreciation of the Life of John David Rheinallt Jones and His Work for the Betterment of Race Relations in Southern Africa*. Johannesburg: Transvaal Printing and Photo-Lithographers, 1953.
Brudholm, Thomas. *Resentment's Virtue: Jean Améry and the Refusal to Forgive*. Philadelphia: Temple University Press, 2008.

Bryant, Alfred T. *Bantu Origins: The People & Their Language.* Cape Town: C. Struik, 1963.
Buthelezi, Mazo Sybil T. MaDlamini. *African Nurse Pioneers in KwaZulu/Natal—1920–2000.* Victoria: Trafford, 2004.
Callaway, Godfrey. *The Fellowship of the Veld: Sketches of Native Life in South Africa.* New York: Negro University Press, 1969.
———. "Further Thoughts about *Ubuntu.*" *The East & the West: A Quarterly Review for the Study of Missionary* 23 (1925): 232–41.
Callaway, Godfrey. *Godfrey Callaway, Missionary in Kaffraria, 1892–1942: His Life and Writings*, edited by E. D. Sedding. London: Society for Promoting Christian Knowledge, 1945.
Callaway, Godfrey. "Manners and Race Relationships." *International Review of Missions* 15, no. 57 (1926): 390–401.
———. *The Soul of an African Padre.* London: A. R. Mowbray, 1932.
Calpin, G. H. et al. *The South African Way of Life: Values and Ideals of a Multi-Racial Society.* New York: Columbia University Press, 1953.
Claassens, Aninka. "People and Whites." *The Black Sash* 28, no. 4 (1986): 18.
Clarke, Liz, and Jane Ngobese. *Women without Men: A Study of 150 Families in the Nqutu District of Kwazulu.* Durban: Institute for Black Research, 1975.
Cochrane, James R. "Salvation and the Reconstruction of Society." In *Happiness, Well-being and the Meaning of Life: A Dialogue of Social Science and Religion*, edited by Vincent Brümer and Marcel Sarot. Kampen: Kok Pharos Publishing House, 1996.
Colenso, John W. *An Elementary Grammar of the Zulu-Kafir Language: Prepared for the Use of Missionaries, and Other Students.* London: Richard Clay, 1855.
Colenso, John W. *Inzindatyana zabantu kanye nezindaba zas'eNatal.* Pietermaritzburg: May and Davis, 1859.
Colenso, John W. *Zulu-English Dictionary.* Pietermaritzburg: P. Davis, 1861.
Constitution of Inkatha Freedom Party, 1996.
Constitution of the Republic of South Africa, Act 108 of 1996.
Constitution of the Republic of South Africa, Act 200 of 1993. http://www.justice.gov.za/trc/legal/sacon93.htm.
Davis T. L. et al. *Village Education in Africa: Report of the Inter-Territorial 'Jeanes' Conference, Salisbury, S. Rhodesia, May 27th–June 6th, 1935.* Lovedale: Lovedale Press, 1936.
De Vries, Egbert. *Man in Community: Christian Concern for the Human in Changing Society.* New York: Association Press, 1966.
Dikoko, D. v T. Z. Mokhatla. No. CCT 62/05. Constitutional Court of South Africa, August 3, 2006. http://www.constitutionalcourt.org.za/Archimages/7541.PDF.
Doke, Clement M. et al. *The Southern Bantu Languages.* London: Dawsons of Pall Mall, 1967.
Doke, Clement M. *Text Book of Zulu Grammar.* London: Longmans, Green and Co., 1945.
Doke, Clement M. "The Earliest Records of Bantu." *Bantu Studies* 12 (1938): 135–44.
Du Plessis, Jacobus A. *IsiXhosa.* Parow: Oudiovista, 1978.
Du Toit, Cornel W. *The Integrity of the Human Person in an African Context: Perspectives from Science and Religion.* Pretoria: Research Institute for Theology and Religion University of South Africa, 2004.
Egenbrecht, J. A. *Zoeloe-leerboek: Met oefeninge, leesstrukke, wordelys en 'n aantal raaisels en spreekwoorde.* Johannesburg: Voortrekkerpers Beperk, 1962.
Elster, Jon. *Closing the Books: Transitional Justice in Historical Perspective.* Cambridge: Cambridge University Press, 2004.
Epstein, A. L. "Injury and Liability: Legal Ideas and Implicit Assumptions." *Mankind* 6, no. 9 (1967): 376–83.
Eze, Michael Onyebuchi. *Intellectual History in Contemporary South Africa.* New York: Palgrave Macmillan, 2010.
Fortes, Meyer. *Religion, Morality and the Person: Essays on Tellensi Religion.* New York: Cambridge University Press, 1987.

Gade, Christian B. N. "The Historical Development of the Written Discourses on *Ubuntu*." *South African Journal of Philosophy* 30, no. 3 (2011): 303–29.
———. "Restorative Justice and the South African Truth and Reconciliation Process." *South African Journal of Philosophy* 32, no. 1 (2013): 10–35.
———. "What is *Ubuntu*? Different Interpretations among South Africans of African Descent." *South African Journal of Philosophy* 31, no. 3 (2012): 484–503.
Gahima, Gerald. *Transitional Justice in Rwanda: Accountability for Atrocity*. London: Routledge, 2013.
Galtung, Johan. "Cultural Violence." *Journal of Peace Research* 27, no. 3 (1990): 291–305.
———. "Violence, Peace, and Peace Research." *Journal of Peace Research* 6, no. 3 (1969): 167–91.
Graybill, Lyn S. *Truth and Reconciliation in South Africa: Miracle or Model?* London: Lynne Rienner Publishers, 2002.
Grout, Lewis. *The Isizulu: A Grammar of the Zulu Language*. Pietermaritzburg: May and Davis, 1859.
———. *The Isizulu: A Revised Edition of a Grammar of the Zulu Language; with an Introduction and Appendix*. London: J. F. Shaw, 1893.
Groves, C. P. *The Planting of Christianity in Africa*. London: Lutterworth Press, 1958.
Hallen, Barry. "'Ethnophilosophy' Redefined?" *Thought and Practice: A Journal of the Philosophical Association of Kenya* 2, no. 1 (2010): 73–85.
Hare, H. H. et al. *I-Testamente entsha yenkosi yetu Ka-Yesu Kristu Gokwamaxosa*. Ishicilelwe Kwisishicilelo Sabra-Wesli: E-Newton Dale, 1846.
Hayner, Priscilla B. *Unspeakable Truths: Transitional Justice and the Challenge of Truth Commissions*, 2nd ed. New York: Routledge, 2011.
Hetherington, Penelope. *British Paternalism and Africa, 1920–1940*. London: F. Cass, 1978.
Hinton, Alexander Laban. "Introduction: Towards an Anthropology of Transitional Justice." In *Transitional Justice: Global Mechanisms and Local Realities after Genocide and Mass Violence*, edited by Alexander Laban Hinton. New Brunswick, NJ: Rutgers University Press, 2011.
Hobbes, Thomas. *Leviathan*. New York: W. W. Norton, 1997.
Hobsbawm, Eric, and Terence Rangers, eds. *The Invention of Tradition*. Cambridge: Cambridge University Press, 1983.
Homer. *Odyssey*. Translated by Stanley Lombardo. Indianapolis, IN: Hackett Publishing Company, 2000.
Hountondji, Paulin J. *African Philosophy: Myth and Reality*. Second Edition. Translated by Henri Evans and Jonathan Rée. Bloomington: Indiana University Press, 1996.
———. "Comments on Contemporary African Philosophy." *Diogenes* 71 (1970): 109–30.
Hume, David. *Essays and Treatises on Several Subjects*, volume 1. London: A. Millar, 1758.
Huntington, Samuel P. *The Third Wave: Democratization in the Late Twentieth Century*. Norman: University of Oklahoma Press, 1991.
Hutchinson, Sharon E. *Nuer Dilemmas: Coping with Money, War, and the State*. Berkeley: University of California Press, 1996.
Iliff, Andrew R. "Root and Branch: Discourses on 'Tradition' in Grassroots Transitional Justice." *The International Journal of Transitional Justice* 6, no. 2 (2012): 253–73.
Institute for Justice and Reconciliation, "Truth, Justice, Memory: South Africa's Truth and Reconciliation Process." Documentary. Cape Town: Institute for Justice and Reconciliation, 2008.
Jabavu, Noni. *Drawn in Colour: African Contrasts*. London: Murray, 1960.
Jordan, A. C. *Tales from Southern Africa*. Berkeley: University of California Press, 1973.
Kagame, Alexis. *La Philosophie Bantu-rwandaise de l'etre*. Brussels: Académie royale des sciences coloniales, 1955.
Kaphagawani, Didier N. "What is African Philosophy?" In *The African Philosophy Reader*, edited by P. H. Coetzee and A. R. J. Roux. London: Routledge, 1998.

Khumalo, Fred. "Drawing Inspiration from the Proud Legacy of Nelson Mandela." Speech delivered to a symposium organized by the Department of Education, Port Elizabeth, September 13, 2008.

Kimenyi, Alexandre. *Studies in Kinyarwanda and Bantu Phonology*. Edmonton: Linguistic Research, 1979.

Kirk, John. *The Economic Aspects of Native Segregation in South Africa*. London: P. S. King & Son, 1929.

Kolini, Emmanuel M., and Peter R. Holmes. *Rethinking Life: What the Church Can Learn from Africa*. Colorado Springs, CO: Authentic Publishing, 2010.

Krige, Eileen J., William John Argyle, and Eleanor Preston-Whyte, eds. *Social System and Tradition in Southern Africa: Essays in Honour of Eileen Krige*. Cape Town: Oxford University Press, 1978.

Krog, Antjie. "'This Thing Called Reconciliation. . . ' Forgiveness as Part of an Interconnectedness-Towards-Wholeness." *South African Journal of Philosophy* 27, no. 4 (2008): 353–66.

Lenta, Patrick. "The Changing Face of the Law: *Ubuntu*, Religion and the Politics of Postcolonial Legality." In *Explorations in Contemporary Continental Philosophy of Religion*, edited by Deane-Peter Baker and Patrick Maxwell. Amsterdam: Editions Rodopi B. V., 2003.

Levy, Philip I. "Sanctions on South Africa: What Did They Do?" Center Discussion Paper, No. 796. Economic Growth Center, Yale University. New Haven, Connecticut, February, 1999.

Lissner, Jørgen. *Namibia 1975: Hope, Fear and Ambiguity*. Geneva: Lutheran World Federation, 1976.

Livingston, William S. *A Prospect of Liberal Democracy*. Austin: University of Texas Bicentennial Committee, 1979.

Lodge, Tom. *South African Politics since 1994*. Cape Town: David Philip Publishers, 1999.

Makgoba, Malegapuru William, ed. *African Renaissance: The New Struggle*. Cape Town: Tafelberg and Mafube, 1999.

Malcolm, D. M. *A Zulu Manual for Beginners: With Exercises*. Cape Town: Longmans, 1960.

Mandela, Nelson. *Long Walk to Freedom*. London: Abacus, 1994.

Marx, Christoph. "Ubu and Ubuntu: On the Dialectics of Apartheid and Nation Building." *Politikon* 29, no. 1 (2002): 49–69.

Marx, Karl, and Frederick Engels. *The German Ideology*, edited by C. J. Arthur. New York: International Publishers, 1970.

Marx, Karl. *Critique of Hegel's "Philosophy of Right,"* edited by Joseph O'Malley. Cambridge: Cambridge University Press, 1982.

Masina, Nomonde. "Xhosa Practices of *Ubuntu* for South Africa." In *Traditional Cures for Modern Conflicts: African Conflict "Medicine,"* edited by William Zartman. London: Lynne Rienner, 2000.

Mayer, Philip. *Black Villagers in an Industrial Society: Anthropological Perspectives on Labour Migration in South Africa*. Cape Town: Oxford University Press, 1980.

Mbeki, Thabo. "Address at the Heritage Day Celebrations." Speech, Taung, North-West Province, September 24, 2005.

———. "Address on the Occasion of Heritage Day." Speech, Cape Town, September 24, 2006.

———. "Address at the Opening of the National House of Traditional Leaders." Speech, City of Tshwane, May 4, 2006.

———. "The African Renaissance, South Africa and the World." Speech at the United Nations University, April 9, 1998.

———. "The African Renaissance Statement." Gallagher Estate, August 13, 1998.

———. "National Tribute in Remembrance of Xenophobic Attacks Victims." Speech, Tshwane, July 3, 2008.

———. "Nelson Mandela Memorial Lecture." Lecture, University of Witwatersrand, July 29, 2006.
———. "Resignation Speech." Address to the people by the South African President, September 21, 2008.
———. "Steve Biko Memorial Lecture." Lecture delivered on the occasion of the thirtieth anniversary of the death of Stephen Bantu Biko, Cape Town, September 12, 2007.
McAuliffe, Padraig. "From Molehills to Mountains (and Myths?): A Critical History of Transitional Justice Advocacy." *Finnish Yearbook of International Law* 22 (2011): 85–166.
McEachern, Charmaine. *Narratives of Nation Media, Memory and Representation in the Making of the New South Africa*. New York: Nova Science Publishers, 2002.
McLaren, James. *A Xhosa Grammar*. Cape Town: Longmans, 1955.
———. "The Wit and Wisdom of the Bantu as Illustrated in Their Proverbial Sayings." *Suid-Afrikaanse Journaal van wetenskap* 14 (1918): 330–44.
Menkiti, Ifeanyi A. "On the Normative Conception of a Person." In *A Companion to African Philosophy*, edited by Kwasi Wiredu. Malden: Blackwell, 2004.
———. "Persons and Community in African Traditional Thought." In *African Philosophy*, edited by Richard A. Wright. New York: University Press of America, 1984.
More, Mabogo P. "African Renaissance: The Politics of Return." *African Journal of Political Science* 7, no. 2 (2002): 61–80.
Motsei, Mmatshilo. *The Kanga and the Kangaroo Court: Reflections on the Rape Trial of Jacob Zuma*. Johannesburg: Jacana, 2007.
Murithi, Timothy. "Practical Peacemaking Wisdom from Africa: Reflections on *Ubuntu*." *The Journal of Pan African Studies* 1, no. 4 (2006): 25–34.
Murray, A. V. *The School in the Bush: A Critical Study of the Theory and Practice of Native Education in Africa*. London: Longmans, 1929.
National Heritage Council. "Building a Nation—Proud of Its African Heritage." Brochure from 2014. http://www.nhc.org.za/wp-content/uploads/2014/03/NHC-Heritage-brochure-A4-Pages.pdf (accessed November 21, 2016).
National Heritage Council. "Ubuntu." Projects on the Website of the National Heritage Council. http://www.nhc.org.za/project/ubuntu/ (accessed November 21, 2016).
Ngcoya, Mvuselelo. "*Ubuntu*: Globalization, Accommodation, and Contestation in South Africa." PhD diss., Faculty of the School of International Service, American University, 2009.
Ngubane, Jordan Kush. *An African Explains Apartheid*. London: Pall Mall Press, 1963.
———. *Conflicts of Minds*. New York: Books in Focus, 1979.
Nietzsche, Friedrich. "History in the Service and Disservice of Life." In *Unmodern Observations*, edited by William Arrowsmith. New Haven: Yale University Press, 1990.
Nkrumah, Kwame. *Consciencism*. London: Heinemann, 1964.
Nurse, Derek. "Bantu Languages." In *Encyclopedia of Language and Linguistics*, edited by Keith Brown, 2nd ed. New York: Elsevier, 2006.
Nyembezi, C. L. S. *Learn More Zulu*. Pietermaritzburg: Shuter and Schooter, 1970.
———. *Zulu Proverbs*. Johannesburg: Witwatersrand University Press, 1963.
Nyerere, Julius. *Freedom and Socialism*. Oxford: Oxford University Press, 1968.
———. *Freedom and Unity*. Oxford: Oxford University Press, 1966.
Ochieng'-Odhiambo, Frederick. *Trends and Issues in African Philosophy*. New York: Peter Lang, 2010.
Oruka, Henry Odera. *Trends in Contemporary African Philosophy*. Nairobi: Shirikon Publishers, 1990.
Paez, Gustavo Rojas. "Retaliation in Transitional Justice Scenarios." In *Handbook of Research on Transitional Justice and Peace Building in Turbulent Regions*, edited by Fredy Cante and Hartmut Quehl. Hershey, PA: Information Science Reference, 2016.

Paton, Alan. *Ah, but Your Land is Beautiful.* New York: Scribner, 1983.
Pauw, B. A. *Christianity and Xhosa Tradition: Belief and Ritual among Xhosa-Speaking Christians.* Cape Town: Oxford University Press, 1975.
———. *The Second Generation: A Study of the Family among Urbanized Bantu in East London.* Cape Town: Oxford University Press, 1973.
P'Bitek, Okot. *African Religions in Western Scholarship.* Nairobi: Kenya Literature Bureau, 1971.
Perrin, James. *An English-Kafir Dictionary of the Zulu-Kafir Language: As Spoken by the Tribes of the Colony of Natal.* Pietermaritzburg: May and Davis, 1855.
Poldervaart, Arie. "Black-Robed Justice in New Mexico." *New Mexico Historical Review* 22, no. 3 (1947): 286–314.
Popper, Karl. *Conjectures and Refutations: The Growth of Scientific Knowledge.* London: Routledge, 1963.
Port Elizabeth Municipality v. Various Occupiers. No.CCT 53/03. Constitutional Court of South Africa, October 1, 2004. http://www.constitutionalcourt.org.za/Archimages/15106.PDF.
Posel, Deborah. "The TRC Report: What Kind of History? What Kind of Truth?" Paper presented at the conference *The TRC: Commissioning the Past*, University of Witwatersrand, 1999.
Poussaint, Renée. *Tutu and Franklin: A Journey Towards Peace.* Documentary. Washington, DC: Wisdom Works, 2001.
Praeg, Leonhard. *African Philosophy and the Quest for Autonomy: A Philosophical Investigation.* Amsterdam: Editions Rodopi, 2000.
Prideaux, S. P. T. "Notes on the Quarterlies." *The Church Missionary Review* 76, no. 849 (1925): 269–71.
Prinsloo, Erasmus D. "*Ubuntu* Culture and Participatory Management." In *The African Philosophy Reader*, edited by Peter Hendrik Coetzee and A. P. J. Roux. London: Routledge, 1998.
Promotion of National Unity and Reconciliation Act, Act 34 of 1995. http://www.justice.gov.za/legislation/acts/1995-034.pdf.
Ramose, Mogobe B. *African Philosophy through Ubuntu.* Harare: Mond Books, 1999.
Reader, D. H. *Zulu Tribe in Transition: The Makhanya of Southern Natal.* Manchester: Manchester University Press, 1966.
Read, Margaret. *Children of their Fathers: Growing up among the Ngoni of Malawi.* New York: Holt, Rinehart and Winston, 1968.
———. *Children of their Fathers: Growing up among the Ngoni of Nyasaland.* London: Methuen, 1959.
Riedel, Johann G. F. *De sluik-en kroesharige rassen tusschen Selebes en Papua.* The Hague: M. Nijhoff, 1886.
Roberts, Charles. *The Zulu-Kafir Language Simplified for Beginners.* London: K. Paul, Trench, Trübner and co., 1895.
———. *The Zulu-Kafir Language Simplified for Beginners.* London: Wesleyan Missionary Society, 1880.
Rodegem, Firmin. *Précis de grammaire rundi.* Brussels: Story-Scientia, 1967.
Ronaldson, Geoffrey K. "Diversity in the Rainbow Nation of South Africa." In *Analysis of Social Interaction Systems: SYMLOG Research and Applications*, edited by A. Paul Hare, Endre Sjøvold, Herbert G. Baker, and Joseph Powers. Lanham: University Press of America, 2005.
Sabra Study Group of Fort Hare. *The Ciskey—A Bantu Homeland: A General Survey.* Fort Hare: Fort Hare University Press, 1971.
Samkange, Stanlake, and Tommie Marie Samkange. *Hunhuism or Ubuntuism: A Zimbabwe Indigenous Political Philosophy.* Salisbury: Graham Publishing, 1980.
———. *The Mourned One.* London: Heinemann Educational, 1975.
Senghor, Léopold. *Pierre Teilhard de Chardin et la politique africaine.* Paris: Editions du Seuil, 1962.

Shaw, Rosalind, and Lars Waldorf, eds. *Localizing Transitional Justice: Interventions and Priorities after Mass Violence*. Stanford: Stanford University Press, 2010.
Shepherd, R. H. W., and B. G. Paver. *African Contrasts: The Story of a South African People*. Cape Town: Oxford University Press, 1947.
Shore, Megan. *Religion and Conflict Resolution: Christianity and South Africa's Truth and Reconciliation Commission*. Farnham: Ashgate, 2009.
Shutte, Augustine. *Ubuntu: An Ethic for a New South Africa*. Pietermaritzburg: Cluster Publications, 2001.
———. "The Common Good Project." Unpublished concept paper from 2000, received in an e-mail from Shutte, December 13, 2010.
Skelton, Ann, and Cheryl Frank. "Conferencing in South Africa: Returning to Our Future." In *Restorative Justice for Juveniles: Conferencing, Mediation and Circles*, edited by Allison Morris and Gabrielle Maxwell. Oxford: Hart Publishing, 2001.
Smith, Edwin William. *The Blessed Missionaries*. Cape Town: Oxford University Press, 1950.
———. *The Way of the White Fields in Rhodesia*. London: World Dominion Press, 1928.
South African Department of Bantu Education. *Xhosa: Terminologie en spelreëls*. Pretoria: Staatsdrukker, 1972.
———. *Zoeloe terminologie en spelreëls*. Pretoria: Staatsdrukker, 1972.
Southern Rhodesian Department of Native Affairs. *NADA: The Southern Rhodesia Native Affairs Department Annual*. Salisbury: Southern Rhodesian Department of Native Affairs, 1950.
Suggit, J., and M. Goedhals. *Change and Challenge: Essays Commemorating the 150th Anniversary of Robert Gray as First Bishop of Cape Town*. Marshalltown: Church of the Province of Southern Africa, 1998.
The State v. Makwanyane and M. Mchunu. No. CCT/3/94. Constitutional Court of South Africa, June 6, 1995. http://www.constitutionalcourt.org.za/Archimages/2353.PDF.
Swanson, Dalene M. "Values in Shadows: A Critical Contribution to Values Education in Our Time." In *International Research Handbook on Values, Education and Student Wellbeing*, edited by Terry Lovat, Ron Toomey and Neville Clement. Dordrecht: Springer, 2010.
Szablewska, Natalia, and Sascha-Dominik Bachmann. "Introduction." In *Current Issues in Transitional Justice: Towards a More Holistic Approach*, edited by Natalia Szablewska and Sascha-Dominik Bachmann. Heidelberg: Springer, 2015.
Teitel, Ruti. "Editorial Note—Transitional Justice Globalized." *The International Journal of Transitional Justice* 2, no. 1 (2008): 1–4.
Teitel, Ruti. "Transitional Justice Genealogy." *Harvard Human Rights Journal* 16 (2003): 69–94.
Tempels, Placide. *Bantu Philosophy*. Translated by Colin King. Paris: Presence Africaine, 1959.
Tharoor, Shashi. *Riot: A Love Story*. New York: Arcade Publishing, 2001.
Thompson, Leonard, and Jeffrey Butler. *Change in Contemporary Africa*. Berkeley: University of California Press, 1975.
Thompson, Leonard. *The Oxford History of South Africa: South Africa to 1870*, volume 1. New York: Oxford University Press, 1969.
Truth and Reconciliation Commission of South Africa Report. Vol. 1–5. Cape Town: Truth and Reconciliation Commission, 1998.
Truth and Reconciliation Commission of South Africa Report. Vol. 6–7. Cape Town: Truth and Reconciliation Commission, 2003.
Tutu, Desmond. *No Future Without Forgiveness*. London: Rider, 1999.
UN Secretary General, *The Rule of Law and Transitional Justice in Conflict and Post-Conflict Societies*, UN Doc. S/2004/616, August 23, 2004.
Valls, Andrew, ed. *Race and Racism in Modern Philosophy*. New York: Cornell University Press, 2005.
Van Binsbergen, Wim. "*Ubuntu* and the Globalization of Southern African Thought and Society." *Quest* 15, no. 1–2 (2001): 53–89.

Van der Merwe, C. G., and Jacques E. du Plessis. *Introduction to the Law of South Africa*. The Hague: Kluwer Law International, 2004.
Van Sembeek, J. *A Bemba Grammar*. London: Longmans, Green and Co., 1955.
Venter, Elza. "The Notion of *Ubuntu* and Communalism in African Educational Discourse." *Studies in Philosophy and Education* 23, no. 2–3 (2004): 149–60.
Vilakazi, Absolom. *Zulu Transformations: A Study of the Dynamics of Social Change*. Pietermaritzburg: University of Natal Press, 1962.
Walker, Oliver. *Kaffirs are Lively: Being some Backstage Impressions of the South African Democracy*. London: V. Gollancz, 1948.
Wamba-dia-Wamba, Ernest. "Philosophy and African Intellectuals: Mimesis of Western Classicism. Ethnophilosophical Romanticism or African Self-Mastery." *Quest* 5, no. 1 (1991), 5–17.
Wilson, Monica H. *Reactions to Conquest: Effects of Contact with Europeans on the Pondo of South Africa*. London: Oxford University Press, 1936.
Wilson, Richard A. *The Politics of Truth and Reconciliation in South Africa: Legitimizing the Post-Apartheid State*. Cambridge: Cambridge University Press, 2001.
Wiredu, Kwasi. "Introduction: African Philosophy in Our Time." In *A Companion to African Philosophy*, edited by Kwasi Wiredu. Malden: Blackwell, 2004.
Wiredu, Kwasi. "Social Philosophy in Postcolonial Africa: Some Preliminaries Concerning Communalism and Communitarianism." *South African Journal of Philosophy* 27, no. 4 (2008): 332–39.
Yamaculo, Incwadi. *Incwadi yamaculo ndawonye nezikungo nezimiselo zekerike yabazalwana, ebizwayo ngokutiwa yeyama-Moravia*. Herrnhut: Fr. Lindenbein, 1885.
Ziervogel, Dirk, Jacobus Abraham Lauw, and J. Ngidi. *A Handbook of the Zulu Language*. Pretoria: J. L. van Schaik, 1976.

Index

abantu. *See* persons
abelungu. *See* whites
Adler, Alfred, 50–51
Africa, narratives of return in, 10–12
An African Explains Apartheid (Ngubane), 67
African humanism, *ubuntu* as, 68
Africanization, 6, 10–11
African National Congress (ANC), 14, 25, 32–33, 83; for change, 9–16; discourse on, 89. *See also* ethnophilosophy; *ubuntu*
African Philosophy Through Ubuntu (Ramose), 63–64, 84–86
African Religions: A Symposium (Booth), 67
African renaissance, 79–83
"The African Renaissance, South Africa and the World" (Mbeki), 79
"African Renaissance: The Politics of Return" (More), 12. *See also Bantu Philosophy*
African Traditional Religious Community, 32
Agrarian Revolution, 11
amnesty, 2–3, 15–16, 25. *See also* Truth and Reconciliation Commission
Amnesty Committee, 2–3, 22
ANC. *See* African National Congress
Annan, Kofi, 2, 19
antiquarian history, xi–xii, 5–6, 78–79, 85
apartheid, 21–22, 25, 62–63. *See also* Sharpeville massacre; Truth and Reconciliation Commission; *ubuntu*
Arendt, Hannah, 14, 16n22
Athens, 19–20
Austin, John L., 6, 85
Aylwin, Patricio, 24

Azanian Peoples Organization and Others v. The President of South Africa and Others, 30–31. *See also Bantu Philosophy*; ethnophilosophy

Bantu Philosophy (*La Philosophie Bantoue*) (Tempels), x–xi, 4, 7n3, 47, 48–53, 89
behavior, of person, 64
Belgian Congo. *See Bantu Philosophy*
Bell, Richard, 23
Bewaji, J. A., 87n35
"The Bewaji, Van Binsbergen and Ramose Debate on *Ubuntu*" (Bewaji and Ramose), 87n35
Biehl, Amy, 33
Biehl, Peter, 33
Biko, Steve, 80
Binsbergen, Van, 6
black community, 33
Black Consciousness, 80
black man, 36
"Black-Robed Justice in New Mexico" (Poldervaart), 26n3
blacks, 47, 62–63
The Black Sash, 62
Black Villagers in an Industrial Society (Mayer), 67
Bloemfontein, South Africa, 31
Booth, Newell Snow, 67
Boraine, Alex, 22–23, 29
Botshabelo, South Africa, 82
Burton, Mary, 34, 35, 36, 40–41
Buthelezi, Mangosuthu, 60, 62–63, 64, 68

change, African philosophy for, 9–16
"Charybdis" (fictional character), 6, 8n25, 85
Chikanda, E. N., 68

Claassens, Aninka, 62
Codesa. *See* Conversation for a Democratic South Africa
colonialism, x–xi, 2
"Comments on Contemporary African Philosophy" (Hountondji), 51–53
community, 33, 60–61
concept of person, 61–64
Conflicts of Minds (Ngubane), 67
Conjectures and Refutations: The Growth of Scientific Knowledge (Popper), 50–51
constitution, 1–2, 14–16, 17n24, 30–31
Constitution of Inkatha Freedom Party (IFP), 17n28
crimes, 39, 60–61
Crossroads, South Africa, 57
cultural enterprise, national reconstruction as, 2, 9
cultural violence, 21–22

da Gama, Vasco, 82
de Klerk, Frederik Willem, 14, 25
democratization, in Spain, 21, 25. *See also* Huntington, Samuel P.; replacements; transplacements
Dias, Bartholomew, 82
direct violence, 21–22
documents, 30–34
du Plessis, Jacques E., 17n24
Durban, South Africa, 32, 65

Einstein, Albert, 50, 51
Elster, Jon, 19–20
Empangeni, South Africa, 33–34
empathy, 57
empirical methods, 4–5
Engels, Friedrich, 85
Enlightenment, x–xi
"The Era of African Renaissance" (Smith), 79
essentialism, x–xii
ethnophilosophy, x–xi, 1, 47–53;
African philosophy in, 7n3;
Hountondji on, x, 4–5, 51–53, 54n34, 55. *See also Bantu Philosophy*; Hountondji, Paulin
Europe, x–xi

Europeans, 11, 47. *See also Bantu Philosophy*; ethnophilosophy
Evans-Pritchard, E. E., 50
Eze, Michael Onyebuchi, 8n22. *See also Intellectual History in Contemporary South Africa*

familyhood (*ujamaa*), 10–11
Finca, Bongani, 38–39, 60, 60–61
forgiveness, *ubuntu*'s link with, 36–39, 40, 57–59
Fortes, Meyer, 63
Franco, Francisco, 21
Frank, Cheryl, 22
Franklin, John Hope, 20
Freedom and Socialism (Nyerere), 10–11
Freud, Sigmund, 50–51

Galtung, Johan, 21
Ghana, 11, 63
Gobodo-Madikizela, Pumla, 36, 57
God, 49, 56, 58, 68
Greece, 19–20
guerrilla forces, 36
Gugulethu, South Africa, 33, 58–59

hearings, 3, 31–34, 35
historicism, x–xii, 77
history, 10, 25–26, 47–53, 50–51, 77–86;
ubuntu and, 65–70, 66, 71n38, 71n41;
written, 65–70, 66, 71n38, 71n41. *See also* antiquarian history
Hlokofa, Cecile, 57–58
Hobbes, Thomas, 12
Hobsbawm, Eric, 25
Homer, 8n25
Homo sapiens, 61–64
Hountondji, Paulin: on African philosophy, xi, xii; on ethnophilosophy, x, 4–5, 51–53, 54n34, 55
How to do Things with Words (Austin), 85
human beings, 56
human rights violations, 19, 21–22, 22, 24, 25. *See also* Burton, Mary; Finca, Bongani; Gobodo-Madikizela, Pumla; Lewin, Hugh; Randera, Fazel

Hunhuism or Ubuntuism: A Zimbabwe Indigenous Political Philosophy (Samkange and Samkange), 5, 12–14, 16n18, 65, 85
Huntington, Samuel P., 3, 24–25
Hutchinson, Sharon, 50

immigrants, 83
India, 20
individual psychology, 50–51
Industrial Revolution, 11
Inkatha Freedom Party (IFP), 15, 17n28, 60
Intellectual History in Contemporary South Africa (Eze), 8n22, 17n28
interconnectedness, 29–30, 59–61, 70
interconnectedness worldview. *See ubuntu*
interim constitution, 1–2, 14–16, 17n24, 30–31
International Center for Transitional Justice, 19
International Journal of Transitional Justice, 19
Introduction to the Law of South Africa (van der Merwe and du Plessis), 17n24
The Invention of Tradition (Hobsbawm and Rangers), 25

justice, 22–24, 26n3. *See also* mob justice; restorative justice; retributive justice; transitional justice

Kaunda, Kenneth, 60
Khumalo, Fred, 62
killings, 57–58, 64. *See also* massacre; murder
Koka, D. K., 32, 33
Krog, Antjie, 1, 4, 29–30, 40, 69
KwaZulu Natal, 61, 62, 64

Lévy-Bruhl, Lucien, 53
Lewin, Hugh, 35
life, history in service of, 77–86
Lodge, Tom, 65

man, 36, 49, 62

Mandela, Nelson, 3, 14, 58, 62, 70, 82
Mandela squatter camp, 32–33
man of action, 5–6, 78, 79–83
Marx, Christoph, 21–22
Marx, Karl, 6, 50–51, 78, 85, 86n13
massacre, 14, 23
Mayer, Philip, 67
Mbeki, Thabo, 3, 14, 84, 85; as man of action, 5–6, 79–83; *ubuntu* highlighted by, 86
Mchunu, Bhekithemba, 61, 64
Menkiti, Ifeanyi A., 63–64
Mgojo, Khoza, 23, 31, 33–34; on Mandela, 58; on *ubuntu*, 36–37, 40, 58, 60
Mitchell, Brian, 23
Mkhwanazi, Jabu, 32
Mlanjeni, Cecil, 57
Mnyakeni, Simon, 32–33
mob justice, 33
Moleke, Leeko, 32
Moral Regeneration Campaign, 81
More, Mabogo P., 12
mothers, 58–59
Mpumalanga, South Africa, 62, 81–82
Mugabe, Robert, 13–14
munhu. *See* persons
murder, 33, 58–59, 64

narratives, 2, 10–12, 16n3. *See also Hunhuism or Ubuntuism: A Zimbabwe Indigenous Political Philosophy*; *ubuntu*
National Question and National Identity Conference, 81–82
national reconstruction, as cultural enterprise, 2, 9
National Ubuntu Imbizo, 82
Nazi regime, 19, 22, 25
négritude, 12
New Mexico, 26n3
Ngubane, Jordan Kush, 65, 67
NHC. *See* National Heritage Council
Nhlapo, 67
Nietzsche, Friedrich, xi–xii, 20–21, 77–86
Nkrumah, Kwame, 11
Ntsebeza, Dumisa, 37–38, 58–59
Nuer Dilemmas (Hutchinson), 50

Nunu, Sindiswa, 58
"Nuremberg or National Amnesia? A Third Way?" (Tutu), 69
Nuremberg trials, 19, 22, 25
Nurse, Derek, 7n20
Nyerere, Julius, 10–11, 56, 80

Odyssey (Homer), 8n25
"Of National Characters" (Hume), 47
On Violence (Arendt), 16n22

past, 20–22
P'Bitek, Okot, x
personhood. *See ubuntu*
persons (*abantu*), 5, 61–64, 69–70. *See also* man
"Persons and Community in African Traditional Thought" (Menkiti), 63–64
Pinochet, Augusto, 24
Poldervaart, Arie, 26n3
politics, 77–86
Popper, Karl, 50–51
Port Elizabeth, South Africa, 62
postcolonial Africa, narratives of return in, 10–12
power, 14, 16n22, 24–25
Praeg, Leonhard, 2, 16n3
Promotion of National Unity and Reconciliation Act, 16, 21, 24, 39
prosecution, as South African possibility, 25
psychoanalysis, 50–51
punishment, 61

racist attitudes, *ubuntu* reducing, 69
Ramose, Mogobe, 6, 63–64, 84–86, 87n35
Randera, Fazel, 35
Rangers, Terence, 25
rapist, 64
Rasool, Ebrahim, 81
rationality, x–xi
reconciliation, 36
religion, 6, 78, 86n13
Reparation and Rehabilitation Committee. *See* Wildschut, Glenda
replacements, 24, 24–25

Report of the Truth and Reconciliation Commission (TRC), 3, 23, 25
Republic of Tanganyika, 10–11
restorative justice, 3, 22–24, 61
"Restorative Justice and the South African Truth and Reconciliation Process" (Gade), 24
retributive justice, 22–24
Riot (Tharoor), 20
ritual incorporation, 63–64
Rousseau, Jean-Jacques, 12. *See also Hunhuism or Ubuntuism: A Zimbabwe Indigenous Political Philosophy*; *Hunhuism or Ubuntuism: A Zimbabwe Indigenous Political Philosophy*

San, 82
Santayana, George, 20
Savage, Beth, 37–38
"Scylla" (fictional character), 6, 8n25, 85
Senegal, 12
Senghor, Léopold, 11–12
Setiloane, Gabriel, 65
Sharpeville massacre, 14
Shutte, Augustine, 80–81, 84
Sidilwane (professor), 31
Skelton, Ann, 22
Smith, Edwin William, 79
socialism, 11
societal change. *See* change
societal transitions, 24–25
sons, 58–59
South Africa, 14–16, 19–26; interim constitution of, 1–2, 17n24, 30–31; villages, 84–86. *See also* apartheid; Truth and Reconciliation Commission; *ubuntu*
South African Constitutional Court, 1–2, 5–6, 15, 30–31
Southern Rhodesia Missionary Conference, 79
static ideas, 47–53
stoning, 64
structural violence, 21

Tanzania, 10–11
Teitel, Rutu, 19

Tempels, Placide, x–xi, 49–51, 55. *See also Bantu Philosophy*
terrorist attack, 58–59
Thaele, Litabe, 32
Tharoor, Shashi, 20
theory, 50–51. *See also Bantu Philosophy*
The Third Wave: Democratization in the Late Twentieth Century (Huntington), 24–25
Tiro, M. A., 31
Tokyo, Japan, 22
torture, 32
TRAC. *See* Transvaal Rural Action Committee
tradition, in transitional justice, 25–26
transitional justice, 2, 19–26, 26n4. *See also* Truth and Reconciliation Commission
transplacements, 24, 25
TRC. *See* Truth and Reconciliation Commission
Trust Feed Massacre, 23
Truth, Justice, Memory: South Africa's Truth and Reconciliation Process, 29
Truth and Reconciliation Commission (TRC), ix, 3, 6n2, 21–22, 22–24, 29–41; establishment of, 16; Investigative Unit, 58–59; *ubuntu* and, 1–4, 25–26, 29–41, 57–58, 86. *See also* Amnesty Committee; Human Rights Violations Committee; Mgojo, Khoza; Wildschut, Glenda; Burton on, 34; hearings led by, 35; Lewin on, 35; *ubuntu* praised by, 4, 23, 29, 31–32, 36, 40, 56, 57, 60, 69

ubuntu, 55–70, 77–86, 89; celebration of, 39; characteristics of, ix–x; in constitution, 1–2, 15–16; definition, 5–6, 30, 40, 66; as displacement narrative, ix–x; in documents, 30–34; forgiveness's link with, 36–39, 40, 57–59; hearings using, 31–34; history and, 65–70, 66, 71n38, 71n41; interviews about, 6n2, 34–39; legitimacy of, xi; as magic discourse, ix–x; as Other's project, x; overview, ix–xii, 5–6; as quality, 66; as reactionary discourse, ix–x; Tutu praising, 4, 23, 29, 31–32, 36, 40, 56, 57, 60, 69; written history of, 65–70, 66, 71n38, 71n41
"*Ubuntu* and the Globalization of Southern African Thought and Society" (van Binsbergen), 84–86
Ubuntu in Nation Building campaign, 82
Ubuntuism. *See Hunhuism or Ubuntuism: A Zimbabwe Indigenous Political Philosophy*
Ubuntu: The Essence of Democracy (Bhengu), 61
ujamaa. *See* familyhood
umuntu. *See* persons
unanimity, x–xii
UNISA. *See* University of South Africa
United Nations University, 79
United Republic of Tanganyika and Zanzibar, 10–11
United Republic of Tanzania, 10–11
University of South Africa (UNISA), 81–82

van Binsbergen, Wim, 5, 65, 84–86, 87n35
van der Merwe, C. G., 17n24
van Riebeeck, Jan, 82
verification, 50–51
Verwoerd, Melanie, 81
villages, 84–86
violations, 20–22
violence, 14, 16n22, 21–22, 33–34, 83

The Way of White Fields: A Survey of Christian Enterprise in Northern and Southern Rhodesia (Smith), 79
Welkom, South Africa, 31–32
Weltanschauung. *See* worldview
Western Cape branch, 58–59
White, John, 79
white community, 33
white man, 36, 62
whites (*abelungu*), 47, 62
Wildschut, Glenda, 4, 34, 35
Wilson, Richard, 3, 26, 56, 85
Wiredu, Kwasi, 2, 9, 63–64
Worcester, South Africa, 31

worldview (*Weltanschauung*), *ubuntu* as, 69. *See also* Nazi regime; Nuremberg trials

xenophobic violence, 83

Zimbabwe, *ubuntu* and creation of, 12–14. *See also Hunhuism or Ubuntuism: A Zimbabwe Indigenous Political Philosophy*; Mugabe, Robert
"Zimbabwe Celebrates Peace Days," 13–14
Zulu royal house, 61

About the Author

Christian B. N. Gade did his PhD on *ubuntu* and restorative justice in post-apartheid South Africa, and he is currently an assistant professor of human security at Aarhus University in Denmark. He specializes in African philosophy and conflict management, and his research on *ubuntu* has been widely read and used. For example, the South African Constitutional Court refers to Gade's research in a judgment (*Everfresh Market Virginia (Pty) Ltd v Shoprite Checkers (Pty) Ltd,* 2011, § 71). In addition to his academic career, Gade works with practical conflict management as a consultant and also as a victim-offender mediator for the Danish police.

www.ingramcontent.com/pod-product-compliance
Lightning Source LLC
Chambersburg PA
CBHW022016300426
44117CB00005B/217